WHEN THE SILENCE BREAKS

A Journey of Healing from Eating Disorders and Sexual Trauma

MONIQUE ONTIVEROS

Copyright © 2025 Monique Ontiveros

All rights reserved.

No part of this book may be reproduced, stored in a retrieval system, or transmitted in any form or by any means—electronic, mechanical, photocopy, recording, or otherwise—without prior written permission of the publisher, except in the case of brief quotations used in reviews or articles.

This is a work of nonfiction. Some identifying details have been changed to protect the privacy of individuals.

Scripture quotations are taken from the NIV Holy Bible. All rights reserved.

Printed in the United States of America.

Cover design by Monique Ontiveros

Paperback ISBN: 979-8-9933863-0-0

The thief comes only to steal and kill and destroy; I have come that they may have life, and have it to the full.

John 10:10

TABLE OF CONTENTS

DEDICATION

To Jesus—who never let go, who called me out of silence and into life.

To my husband and children—you are living reminders of God's redemption and the joy He restores.

And to every reader carrying hidden pain—may you find healing, hope, and freedom in the One who calls you beloved.

8

TRIGGER WARNING

This book contains descriptions of sexual abuse, trauma, eating disorders, self-harm, and suicidal ideation. These topics are shared with honesty and vulnerability to shed light on the healing and redemption available through Jesus. Please care for your heart as you read, and feel free to pause or seek support if needed.

When the Silence Breaks

Dear Reader,

It is not by accident that you are reading this book. Whether you're battling an eating disorder, an addiction, the trauma of sexual abuse, or simply struggling to find your worth, I invite you to walk this journey with me. I have been where you are—feeling broken, trapped by shame, and questioning whether healing is even possible. I had spent years searching for peace in all the wrong places, and it wasn't until I encountered Christ's unconditional love that I truly began healing.

This book is my personal story, but it might also be your story. It's for anyone who has felt lost, hopeless, or damaged by life's deepest wounds. My prayer is that, through my story, you may discover your true identity—the identity that God Himself has given you. In these pages, you'll find not only my testimony but also the powerful, life-giving truths of scripture that helped me reclaim my life. Without a doubt, these God-given truths can help you reclaim yours as well because if God helped me, He would do the same for you.

No matter where you are on your journey, this book offers hope. There is freedom waiting for you, and it begins with understanding who you are in Christ. I believe that as you read, God will reveal His love, heal your heart, and equip you to fight the spiritual battles you face.

You are not defined by your past, and you are not alone. Together, let us walk through the healing, the battles, and the victories that are only possible through Christ. I urge you to embrace the freedom, peace, and purpose that He has for you.

With love and hope,
Monique Ontiveros

Introduction:

My Story

The devil is a liar.

I was 22 years old. It was late. The house was quiet, but my thoughts are deafening. I was locked in the bathroom, crumpled on the cold tile floor, sobbing so hard I could barely breathe. My mom and two younger sisters were in the other room, the one I share with my sisters, and

I knew they could hear me. But nothing could reach the war raging within me.

The bathroom—the only bathroom in our two-bedroom house—had become my hiding place. I had locked myself in there so many nights before, hurting myself in silence, cutting in places no one could see. My mom eventually caught on and started hiding every sharp object in the house. Even the knives were kept in a locked drawer. But that night, as I was sobbing, crumpled on the bathroom floor, I remembered one she missed. At the back of her desk drawer was a blade—one of those tiny, rectangular, single-edge scraper blades.

I got up and ran, barefoot, down the hallway and into Mom's bedroom. I beelined to her desk and yanked open the drawer. My fingers wrapped around cold steel. But before I could use it, my mom came flying into the room. She threw herself on me and tackled me to the floor, yelling to my sister to take the blade. I screamed and sobbed as she pinned me down, refusing to let me go. My sister rushed in and tore the blade from my hand.

It was then that I heard her words; through her own tears, my mom began whispering, "The devil is a liar." Over and over, she uttered those words, like a battle cry wrapped in love.

As she did, something broke open in me, and I whispered, "I don't want this to be my story anymore." Words only God and I knew I uttered.

That night, I surrendered. What was supposed to be the end, and it felt like it was, turned into a beginning of something beautiful.

But to understand what brought me to that floor that night, we need to go back.

Before the hospitals.

Before the eating disorder.

Before the assault.

Before the police station.

I was eight years old the first time I can remember that he touched me. My uncle. My father's brother. Someone I was supposed to trust. I didn't understand what was happening. All I knew was that it made me feel small, scared, and ashamed. It didn't stop. Year after year since then, it had become a silent part of my world. I learned to freeze. Not fight. Not run. Just stay still and wait for it to be over.

This coping mechanism followed me into adolescence. It felt like safety then, but it became a chain that held me hostage. Even in moments when I wanted to say no, when I needed to speak, I couldn't, as though even my voice had abandoned me.

My family moved constantly. By the time I was fifteen, I'd lost track of how many schools I had been to. Each move felt like a fresh start on the outside but deepened my isolation on the inside. I didn't let anyone in. I didn't get too close. No one stayed in my life long enough to notice what was happening behind closed doors—and that's exactly how I wanted it.

But once, I slipped.

In middle school, I broke down crying during lunch. The night before, as I was trying to sleep, my uncle visited my bedroom again. That morning, I woke up and got ready for school in a daze, questioning myself. Did that really happen again? Was it all a nightmare? I questioned myself, but I knew the truth, only it's a truth I didn't want to believe. A girl in my class, one I trusted, asked what was wrong. For the first time, I told someone about my uncle. Not everything, but enough.

The girl told the school counselor, who called my parents. That night, my parents sat me down, voices shaky, eyes wide with fear. It was my chance to speak the truth. But I didn't. I lied. I told them it was a misunderstanding. That nothing had happened. I denied everything.

I was terrified. Not just of what might happen to me but of what might happen to him as well. I wanted to protect my family; I wanted to protect him. I told myself I was doing the right thing. But I was wrong, because I was protecting the one who had been hurting me when I shouldn't.

I never spoke to that girl again. I was furious with her for telling, like she had betrayed me. She broke my trust, which I don't often give freely to anyone. But I know now—she was trying to help. She saw my pain and did the only thing she could. But I wasn't ready. I thought silence was safer.

That silence bled into everything.

By the time I was in high school, the pain was unbearable and anorexia was making me disappear to into a walking skeleton. In ninth grade, my English teacher stepped in. She handed me a list of school clubs and gently encouraged me to find a place where I could belong. I barely glanced at the paper until a certain club name caught my eye: The Cause. Later, I learned that it was a Christian group that met once a week during lunch. I didn't bother looking at the other options.

I walked into my first meeting with The Cause unsure of what to expect. But I clearly remember how it felt from the moment I entered that classroom and soon learned more about the group—it felt different. Safe. Warm. The Cause only had around 15 members, but they were all kind. They prayed. They believed. I didn't fully understand it, but something about being in The Cause felt right. A heaviness I wasn't even aware I was carrying was lifted off my shoulders, and it felt like I could actually breathe.

I didn't know it then, but now I know it was the Holy Spirit.

That day became a turning point. I kept going back—week after week, year after year. I stuck with The Cause for all of high school. I soaked up everything I could about God, about Scripture, about truth. I started believing, at least in my mind, that there was more to life than pain. That there was a God who saw me.

But my heart remained chained. The shame. The silence. The lie that I was damaged beyond repair still clung to me.

Then came the police station.

The day before my 18th birthday, my mom picked me up from school. Her eyes were rimmed red. Her hands clutched the steering wheel like she was bracing for impact. "We're going to the police station," she said softly.

My stomach dropped. I didn't want to go. I didn't want to speak. I didn't want my uncle—the man who had been abusing me for over a decade—to get in trouble. He was my dad's brother. Someone my family loved. Someone I had loved too, in a twisted, confused way.

But the truth was out now. My parents finally knew. I finally told them. Not everything but enough for my mom to take me to the police station. It happened after my pediatrician had reported my case. During a visit with my pediatrician, I opened up to her. I didn't really know what gave me confidence to finally share my story, but I really liked her.

When I told my parents, I remember being done with the abuse. All I could think of was how my uncle had touched me and threatened me too many times, and I was done.

I sat in that station, pen trembling in my hand, and signed my name. Not as a child, but as someone stepping into adulthood in the most unimaginable way. These weren't the papers I pictured starting my adult life with.

I wish I could say things got better after that, but it felt more like the beginning of a storm than the end of one.

My uncle disappeared after the report. Gone without a trace. But his absence didn't erase the years of damage he left behind. I didn't know then that he wouldn't be the last to break my trust and my spirit.

The summer before college, I enjoyed going to the park in the neighborhood, where I played ball with some kids. It was like having a semblance of a life. Until one day, I went with two boys I thought were my friends. One of them suddenly looked at me and said, "We have to do this before you leave to college as a virgin."

I froze.

My trauma response kicked in. My body shut down. I couldn't move, couldn't speak, couldn't fight. And once again, I let something happen that I didn't want, because I didn't know how to make it stop.

I walked home in silence, crawled into bed, and stared at the ceiling in numb disbelief. I wrote on my wall: "Jesus is all I have and need."

And I meant it. But I was crushed.

I left for college hoping to escape it all. But the loneliness followed me. My eating disorder worsened, and depression swallowed me. I survived on walks, gym sessions, and one tiny salad a day—topped with pepper for flavor instead of dressing. I was disappearing.

But even then, God pursued me.

I met this woman who did a lot of outreach programs and clubs in our campus. She was kind and always prayed with me, and became the first person in years to consistently show up for me. She discipled me and eventually baptized me.

I had hoped the pain would stay buried in the water I left behind. But the lies still lingered.

I began drinking and smoking to cope. It numbed the ache for a while but only deepened my shame. Despite getting into a university that I had fought hard for, I couldn't keep up. I spiraled. Eventually, I was labeled a threat to myself and was forced to leave because my eating disorder was completely taking over.

I spent the next three years in and out of hospitals—first full hospitalization, then partial programs. Therapy helped me survive, but it didn't heal me. The battle wasn't just in my mind; it was in my spirit.

At 21, I left the hospital and turned to fitness. It became my new obsession. I went on long walks, and I trained hard.

I've always been athletic, but this time, when I signed up for kickboxing, I felt strong for the first time in a long time. But strength doesn't always mean safety.

A fellow class attendant started showing interest. He invited me to a party and we drank. He told me he was tired and needed to lie down. I told him I didn't want to have sex. "We're not," he said. He lied.

I followed him into a dark room, feeling uneasy and honestly scared. It was that time of the month for me, and I was wearing a tampon. And still, he took advantage of me. My body froze. My mind shut down. I cried out to God silently in my head: "Please make this end. Please make this end."

Afterward, I ran to the restroom, where I remained for a long time. Completely in disbelief of what just happened and frantically trying to remove the tampon, which had been painfully lodged up where it should not be. I somehow convinced myself I had to make the relationship work now, thinking if I stayed, it would undo the shame. This guy, still a stranger to me, suddenly held some kind of grip over me. But the abuse didn't end night.

Then came the accident.

I was the passenger while he drove us around a city, hours from home, when it happened. I wasn't even supposed to be with him, but he said he didn't want to drive by himself; he needed to drive up there for work. I didn't see it coming. One moment I was watching a movie on my phone while he drove, the next I opened my eyes, and the grill of a big Tahoe truck was to the right side of my face. I blacked out.

That violent car crash left me with broken bones, a partially collapsed lung, and shattered teeth. I should have died, but I didn't.

I believe God used that crash to rip me out of that toxic relationship. To separate me physically from the person who was still hurting me. But even then, the pain didn't stop. I started smoking and drinking even more to escape. Then, when I found out he had been unfaithful—something I suspected anyways—I snapped.

That was the night I tried to take my life.

The night I was tackled to the floor.

The night the blade was ripped from my hand.

The night my mom held me and whispered through tears: "The devil is a liar."

That night, I surrendered everything to God. I told Him I didn't want to be defined by trauma or anorexia anymore. I didn't want to carry the shame. I didn't want the silence, the lies, the cycles. I laid it all down.

Slowly, God began rebuilding me. Mark 5:41 became my anthem: "Little girl, I say to you, get up."

Though this story begins in darkness, it's not where it ends. God's light broke through. He rescued me. He healed me. He renamed me. He gave me purpose.

If you've ever felt trapped in shame…

If you've ever wondered if healing is possible…

If you've ever wanted to give up…

Just know, you are not alone.

There is freedom.

There is healing.

There is hope.

And His name is Jesus.

This is my story of His relentless love and the freedom I found in Him.

1

Marked by His Image: Imago Dei

I am broken but not worthless.

For most of my life, I believed this lie. It was a lie that seeped into my mind early on, making me believe I was worthless, broken beyond repair, and that somehow, everything that happened to me was my fault. From the age of eight, when my uncle began molesting me, to the repeated assaults and abuse I endured as a young adult, this lie shaped the way I saw myself.

I thought my worth was gone, stolen by the abuse. I thought I was dirty and impure. I thought I could never be whole again.

As a child, I didn't have the words to explain the trauma I was experiencing. I just knew that something was wrong. What should have been a carefree childhood became a prison of shame and secrecy.

My uncle, a person who should have protected me, used his power to manipulate and silence me. For ten years, I lived under the weight of his abuse. When I was 18, I had been assaulted by multiple young men. The final blow came when I was raped at 21, falling into a new cycle of abuse. I remember thinking, *This is my life. This is the cycle I'll live in forever.* I thought this curse, this brokenness, would replay for the rest of my life, no matter what I did.

At 12, I developed an eating disorder to control the one thing I thought I could—my body. Anorexia became my slow way out, a way to shrink myself into nothingness. I believed that if I died from it, I'd be a "successful" anorexic.

When I was in the hospital for my eating disorder, I told my psychiatrist, "I'm the problem. All these things keep happening to me, and I'm the common denominator, so I must be the issue."

No amount of therapy or medication could stop the pain or the pattern. I believed I would never escape, that I would never be worthy of love, marriage, or even a normal life.

I thought, I am just a sex object to be used, no one will ever see me for anything else.

This belief shaped years of my life. I spiraled into depression, overwhelming thoughts, and eventually self-harm.

THE NIGHT EVERYTHING CHANGED

You're too far gone. Nothing will ever change. You're worthless. These lies had filled my head until it became too much, and I couldn't bear it any longer. I had reached the end of myself. Anorexia had taken almost everything, but even that wasn't enough anymore. I was ready to end my life.

That was the night of my suicide attempt. The night that changed everything.

But my mother's words pierced through the noise.

I wouldn't call my mother a devout Christian, but she knew God, and she understood what was happening to me. My mother knew I was letting the lies of the devil get through to me. So, with her small, tattooed frame, she embraced me tightly, holding me as though telling the devil she won't let me go. And she didn't. Her small voice reached my soul, and over and over, she whispered, "The devil's a liar."

A revelation hit me. For the first time, I saw the battle for what it was—a spiritual war for my soul. The devil had been whispering lies into my mind for years, keeping me bound in shame, guilt, and self-hatred. But in that moment, I saw the truth: those were lies, and so they couldn't be from God. They were from the enemy, and I had been believing them for far too long. I had let the enemy's lies have a hold on me, but no more.

Through tears, I broke down and cried out to God, telling Him, "I don't want this anymore. I don't want this to be my identity." In that moment, I released my grip on anorexia, my pain, my trauma—everything I had been clinging to. I told myself, if I want this later, I can always go back. But for now, I'm letting everything go.

That night, I sobbed myself to sleep in my mom's arms. When I woke up the next day, something had shifted. I felt lighter, as if the heaviness I'd been carrying for years had been lifted. For the first time in a long time, I wanted to fight—not against myself, but *for* myself.

LEARNING THE TRUTH: IMAGO DEI

My journey to healing wasn't immediate. Believing the truth about who I truly was, who I was to God, wasn't easy, and it took time. I had spent years believing I was worthless, and suddenly, I was learning a new truth: I was made in the image of God.

The more I read scripture and listened to teachings, the more God showed me what that meant. Being created in

His image wasn't just a mere motivational phrase—it was the foundation of my identity. It meant I wasn't defined by what had been done to me or by the choices I'd made. It meant I was loved, valued, and had a purpose.

For years, I found it hard to believe that this truth applied to me. How could someone as broken as I was reflect the image of a perfect God? In Matthew 5:48, Jesus instructed His followers to be perfect as our heavenly Father is perfect. Even Deuteronomy 32:4 mentioned God's perfection. It says that His works are perfect and His ways are just. He is faithful and does no wrong. He is a just and upright God.

It was not easy to wrap my head around the idea that I was created in His likeness. But the more I leaned into His Word, the more He showed me that my worth wasn't based on my perfection. It was intrinsic, because He created me in His image, and nothing could take that away.

FIGHTING THE LIES WITH TRUTH

The lies didn't disappear overnight. There were moments I still felt broken and worthless. Sometimes, I felt tempted to go back to the eating disorder and self-harm, especially during emotional struggles. But whenever I tried, the lies that used to chain me felt strange. It didn't feel the same. The lies didn't fit anymore, like trying to wear a shoe two sizes too small.

The past still haunted me sometimes, but my perspective had changed the moment I started believing God's word, and He started showing me my real identity.

Psalms 139:13-14

13 For you created my inmost being, you knit me together in my mother's womb.
14 I praise you because I am fearfully and wonderfully made; your works are wonderful; I know that full well.

When lies crept in, I ran to God's word. His word reminded me of who I truly was, as stated in the verses above: fearfully and wonderfully made. These truths became my anchor, and the way I fought back against the enemy.

SEEING MYSELF THROUGH HIS EYES

Healing was messy. Surrendering my life to God didn't mean everything was suddenly perfect. Battles were still ahead of me. But something inside me had already shifted. I no longer carried the identity of trauma, self-harm, and shame. Instead, I began seeing myself through the lens of His love.

Before, when I looked at my reflection in the mirror, I always struggled with what I saw. My appearance wasn't something I was happy with. I even described my body as boyish, not having any feminine curves. But more than that, past all the physical features, I saw a broken woman.

But as I continued meditating on God's word, God made me see what He saw—who I really was. I began seeing a new image. I wasn't defined by my past. I wasn't defined by the pain. I was defined by the truth that I was made in God's image and that He had a purpose for my life.

This realization changed everything. And I know it can change everything for you too. Let me ask you something: When you introduce yourself, what comes to mind? What's the inner dialogue that follows your name?

Is it "I'm a mom," "I've been through a lot," or "I'm just trying to get by?"

Maybe it's, "I'm divorced," or "I have anxiety," or "I've made mistakes."

Sometimes we attach our identity to our circumstances or experiences, but our circumstances are not our identity.

Your trauma isn't your name tag.
Your past isn't your calling card.
Your struggle isn't your definition.
You are who God says you are.

When He formed you, He didn't stamp "anxious," "addict," "unworthy," or "damaged" across your soul. He stamped "image-bearer," "loved," "known," and "crafted with purpose." That's who you've always been, even before you ever believed it.

When I finally surrendered, *really* surrendered, I began to see the truth, which was not what the enemy wanted me to believe. Not what my past said about me, but what my Creator had declared from the beginning, even before I was formed in my mother's womb.

I wasn't created to be consumed by shame, or to punish my body, or hide my pain. I wasn't created to chase perfection or earn love.

I was created to reflect Him, to carry His light, to walk in truth and freedom, and to live fully, knowing I bear the fingerprints of the Father.

The enemy does not fear who you used to be; he fears who you could become if you know who you are. That's why he fights so hard to distort the image.

To lie.
To distract.
To cover.
To kill the seed of identity before it can take root.

But God restores what's been stolen. And for me, He began with one powerful truth: You are Mine. You bear My image. You were made to reflect My glory.

That didn't mean I was healed instantly. It didn't mean I never struggled again. But it gave me a starting place. A foundation. A reason to fight differently. When you know you were made in His image; you stop treating yourself like a mistake. You stop letting shame speak louder than grace.

I began eating again, not to gain weight, but to gain life.
I began looking in the mirror, not for flaws, but for fingerprints.
I began opening my heart, not in fear, but in faith.

Imago Dei means we are not random. We are not worthless. We are not forgotten.

It means your story—yes, your story—is sacred.

Because you are sacred.

I don't know what lies have been chasing you. I don't know what mirrors you've been standing in front of, or what messages you've been absorbing from the world or your past. I do know this: nothing can erase the image of God from your life.

Not the eating disorder. Not the abuse.
Not the choices you regret.
Not the nights you've cried yourself to sleep.

Not even the voices that still whisper, "you're not enough."

Because He is enough. And He made you in His image.

So today, I invite you to believe again. To look at your life not through the lens of pain, but through the truth of Genesis 1:27.

It says,

So God created mankind in his own image, in the image of God he created them; male and female he created them.

You are fearfully and wonderfully made. You were handcrafted by the Creator of the universe. You were meant to carry His likeness, and you still do.

Even if you feel broken—especially if you feel broken—remember: you are His.

And His image never fades.

REFLECTION: IMAGO DEI

RESPOND

1. Who are you? When you introduce yourself, even silently, what words come to mind?
2. Have you been defining yourself by your past or your pain more than by the truth of God's Word?
3. What would it look like to start your days believing you are an image-bearer of God?

MEDITATION

Take a moment to think about the areas in your life where you feel broken. It could be pain from your past, wounds you haven't fully acknowledged, or lies you've believed about yourself.

Now ask yourself: What does God see when He looks at me?

The answer may surprise you. He doesn't see your brokenness as a flaw—He sees it as a canvas for His redemption. The same God who created the universe chose to create you in His image, calling you "fearfully and wonderfully made" (Psalm 139:14).

When I started seeing my brokenness through God's eyes, I expected judgment, but instead, He showed me love and beauty. It wasn't immediate, and it wasn't easy, but slowly, I began to understand that my worth wasn't tied to what I had been through. It was tied to Him.

1 John 1:6 says, "If we claim to have fellowship with him and yet walk in the darkness, we lie and do not live out the truth." For so long, I had been living in the darkness brought by the lies that kept me bound to shame and pain. As I embraced God's truth, I realized He was calling me out of darkness and into His marvelous light. Walking in truth doesn't happen overnight, but every small step toward His light brings us closer to healing and freedom.

PRACTICING THE TRUTH

Now that you've reflected on who you are in Christ, the next step is to walk in that truth every day. Living your life believing you are created in His image will always be an ongoing process, but you can start with small, intentional actions that will align your life with God's Word. Here are a few ways to begin:

1. **Renew Your Mind Daily.** Replace lies with truth by meditating on scripture. Write down specific lies you've believed and pair them with corresponding verses that remind you of who you are in Christ.

2. **Speak Truth Over Yourself.** Stop negative self-talk and affirm God's truth in your words. Declare promises like "He has plans to prosper you and not to harm you" (Jeremiah 29:11), "I am fearfully and wonderfully made" (Psalm 139:14), or "By His wounds, I am healed" (Isaiah 53:5).

3. **Walk in Integrity.** Let your actions reflect God's truth. Make decisions based on His Word, not on fear or shame. Be honest, even when it's hard, and ask for forgiveness when you stumble.

4. **Stay in Fellowship.** Surround yourself with people who encourage you in your faith. Join a small group or Bible study, and let trusted friends hold you accountable.

5. **Trust God Through Obedience.** Take steps of faith as He leads you. Surrender areas of control, and let His Word guide your choices.

6. **Celebrate Progress.** Recognize that healing and transformation take time. Thank God for every small victory and extend grace to yourself when you fall short.

As you practice these steps, remember that God's love and grace are constant. Even when it feels messy or hard, He is with you, guiding you toward freedom and wholeness. These aren't just disciplines, they are declarations.

JOURNAL ENTRY

Before you begin writing, speak this truth out loud:

"I am created in the image of God. My brokenness does not define me. God sees beauty in me because I am His creation. Through Him, I find healing and purpose."

In your journal, write a letter to yourself from God's perspective, beginning with these words:

"My beloved child, you bear My image…"

Let God's words affirm your identity, confront any lies you've believed, and restore what's been lost. Don't worry about getting it "right," just be honest, and let the Holy Spirit lead you.

45

PRAYER

Father,

Thank You for creating me in Your image.

Thank You that nothing I've been through—no trauma, no mistake, no label—can erase the truth that I belong to You.

Help me see myself the way You see me: loved, chosen, and made with purpose.

When the lies creep in, teach me to run to Your Word, to speak truth over myself, and to walk in the identity You've given me.

I surrender the false names I've carried—shame, fear, failure—and I receive the name You speak over me: Mine. May Your truth take root in my heart and grow deeper every day.

In Jesus' name,

Amen.

2

A New Creation: Living From the Inside Out

Something shifted and now, I am new.

In the last chapter, we explored how God created us in His image, that His fingerprints have been on us from the very beginning. But God didn't just create us; He also made a way to redeem us. We're not just image-bearers—we're also new creations, transformed by the power of Christ. This chapter is about learning how to live with that new identity.

The morning after I surrendered my pain to God, something was different. It wasn't that all the hurt had vanished or that everything in my life was suddenly perfect, but I felt a flicker of hope. For years, I had carried the weight of shame, trauma, and the belief that I was too broken to be made whole. I believed I was my eating disorder. But that morning, something shifted. The lies that had wrapped themselves around my identity began to unravel. It was as if, for the first time, I could see a path forward, and I was ready to step onto it. I was ready to fight—not myself, but *for* myself. I knew it was not because of anything I had done, but of what Jesus had already done for me.

I used to think that being a new creation meant behaving better and performing better. I thought it was all about earning a fresh start, so I had spent so much time trying to fix myself. But the gospel doesn't work like that.

2 Corinthians 5:17 says:

Therefore, if anyone is in Christ, he is a new creation. The old has passed away;
behold, the new has come.

I had read this verse countless times, but only now did I truly understand the apostle Paul meant. I wasn't being remodeled; I was being reborn. I was being given a new identity. A new beginning.

New creation doesn't mean I forget my past. It doesn't erase everything I've been through. It means those things no longer get to define me; Christ does. Becoming new in Christ isn't about amnesia, but about authority. The old me still tries to whisper sometimes, but now, I have the truth to answer back.

THE OLD HAS PASSED AWAY

"I am not who I was," I declared one day while I was looking at myself in the mirror. It felt awkward. But it also felt powerful. That was the moment I began walking differently, not because my circumstances had changed, but because my identity had. More accurately, I had reclaimed my true identity—the one God had given me. I stopped letting my past name me or have power over me. I stopped letting the pain of what was done to me shape who I believed I was.

The enemy's strategy is simple: if he can't keep you in your past, he'll try to convince you that nothing's changed. He will always remind you of your pain, of your shame, and of your experiences, highlighting your messes. But remember, the devil is a liar, and this is just one of his lies. Something has changed; you've already been made new. You're not becoming a new creation—you already are. The challenge is learning how to live with that truth.

Sometimes, the hardest part is letting go of the old. The labels I previously carried felt like the truth. Letting go of them was not easy, and it was terrifying because it meant I had to face the unknown. If I wasn't defined by my eating disorder or trauma or addictions, then who was I? I had to release the narratives that said I was too far gone, too messed up, or too broken. Letting go wasn't denial; it was declaration. It was a decision to believe what God says over what my trauma or my old self screamed. As I did this, I discovered something beautiful: God was there, waiting to meet me in the middle of my mess and lift me up. He was there to help me change the narratives I used to believe in.

He was there to introduce me to the "me" that He created me to be.

Romans 12:2 became my guiding verse as I go through this transformation. I had it written on my wall to keep it in front of my eyes and meditate on it often.

It says,

Do not conform to the pattern of this world, but be transformed by the

renewing of your mind.

I realized that although I was already a new creation, the transformation I was seeking didn't just happen once—it was (and still is) a process. Old habits don't die overnight, and even as a "new creation," we might still find ourselves with them. The old lies from the enemy were our truth for a long time. As a new creation with old lies still lingering in us, we are like new wineskins trying to hold old wine. It doesn't fit, so we should make sure that we are carrying a new wine every day because we are a new wineskin. Each day I choose truth, and each time I speak life instead of shame, I walk further into the new creation I already am.

Luke 5:37-39 says,

> [37] *And no one pours new wine into old wineskins. Otherwise, the new wine will burst the skins; the wine will run out and the wineskins will be ruined.*
> [38] *No, new wine must be poured into new wineskins.* [39] *And no one after drinking old wine wants the new, for they say, 'The old is better.'"*

One practice I learned, which I still apply to this day, is to replace every lie or negative thought I speak or think towards myself with at least three truths from the Word of God. It was challenging at first, but the more I did it, the quicker and easier it became to know God's truths and fully believe them. I noticed how the number of times I spoke harshly about myself lessened until it hardly happens at all.

Here are some few truths that I clung to as I rewrote the self-talk:

> **1. I am a new creation in Christ** (2 Corinthians 5:17). My past no longer defines me. I am made new, and my identity is rooted

in who God says I am, not in what has happened to me or what I have done.

2. I am loved and chosen by God (Ephesians 1:4-5). The enemy tried to convince me that I was unworthy of love, but God's Word reminds me that I am chosen, loved, and adopted into God's family.

3. I am forgiven and redeemed (Colossians 1:13-14). No matter what mistakes I made or how deeply I felt the shame of my past, I am forgiven. Christ's sacrifice has redeemed me, and I am free from the weight of sin.

4. I am fearfully and wonderfully made (Psalm 139:14). When God created me in my mother's womb, He created someone wonderful. I do not agree with the lie of the enemy that I was made by mistake or made wrong.

As I continue on this journey, I've noticed something else—God uses my story to help others find their way too.

That's the beauty of becoming a new creation. It doesn't just change your life; it becomes a light for someone else's. You get to say, *"I've been there. I've lived through the dark. But Jesus brought me into the light, and He'll do the same for you."*

REFLECTION: EMBRACING THE NEW CREATION

RESPOND

1. What "old things" have you been holding onto as if they're still part of you? Which ones do you think would be the hardest to let go?

2. Have you ever believed that being a new creation means feeling "fixed" instead of truly changed? If yes, do you still believe the same thing? If not, what changed?

3. How would your thoughts and actions shift if you fully believed you are already new in Christ?

PRACTICING THE TRUTH

It's hard to let go of the old, but in order to move forward, you need to fully accept that you are now a new creation, and therefore, must act like one.

The following are some guides to help you embrace the new creation that is you:

1. **Start With Scripture:** Meditate on 2 Corinthians 5:17 daily.

   "Therefore, if anyone is in Christ, he is a new creation. The old has passed away; behold, the new has come."

2. **Speak Identity Over Behavior:** Declare, "This is not who I am anymore; I am a new creation."

3. **Journal Your Growth:** Track spiritual milestones and breakthroughs.

4. **Let Go of Shame Stories:** Stop rehearsing what God has already redeemed.

5. **Surround Yourself with Life-Givers:** Spend time with people who speak truth over your identity.

JOURNAL PROMPT

Start your journal entry today with this line:

"Because I am a new creation, I no longer have to…"

Write freely. Name the old things you're letting go of and declare the new life you're stepping into.

Close your journal entry with this statement:

"I am not who I was. I am not what I've done. I am who God says I am—made new, made whole, and made for more."

59

PRAYER FOR RENEWAL AND PURPOSE

Father,

Thank You for the promise that in Christ, I am a new creation. Thank You that the old no longer defines me, and I am free to walk in the new. Help me let go of the things in my past that still hold me back. Renew my mind daily and remind me of the truth of who I am in You. Give me the strength to fight the lies of the enemy and to embrace the new life You've given me.

Fill my heart with Your purpose and use my story to bring hope to others. Thank You for Your love, grace, and the new beginning You've offered me.

In Jesus name,

Amen.

3

Escaping the Shadows of Shame— Finding Freedom from Guilt and Shame

What if they think I'm disgusting?

What if they don't believe me?

What if I'm just too broken?

These questions used to run through my head, keeping me from speaking up. There's a silence that shame brings. It's the kind that doesn't just quiet your voice—it crushes it. I know that silence well. I lived in it for years.

It was the reason it took me a decade until I talked about my uncle's abuse to someone. Sometimes, I wonder what would have happened if I had spoken sooner? Would I have been a different person now? Would it have stopped the abuse that happened to me throughout the years? Would I have had better relationships with people, and even romantic ones?

I used to think I was too broken to deserve love, and I was too consumed with guilt and shame to speak up.

Even after surrendering to Jesus, I still struggled to speak up. I'd start sharing and then pull back.

Shame has a way of convincing us that our past disqualifies us from our future. It whispers that we're too far gone. Too dirty. Too different.

So instead of healing, we hide.
Instead of freedom, we fake it.
Instead of connection, we isolate, trying to look put together while falling apart inside.

For years, shame was my constant companion. It lingered over me, casting shadows on every aspect of who I was and how I saw myself. Shame told me that everything that had happened to me was somehow my fault. It whispered that the abuse I suffered as a child, the assaults, and the decisions I made to cope were evidence of my brokenness and unworthiness. And as long as I believed those lies, shame had a powerful grip on me.

But shame isn't from God. It's a weapon the enemy uses to keep us trapped in a cycle of self-condemnation, guilt, and fear. It makes us too focused on our mistakes, too consumed by the belief that we're unworthy of love and forgiveness. That's exactly where I was. I was convinced that my past disqualified me from God's grace. For the longest time, I believed I was damaged goods.

Because of the abuse.

Because of the eating disorder.

Because of the choices I made when I was lost and hurting.

DAMAGED, NOT DISQUALIFIED

I never had a good relationship with people. I always felt too broken and too worried they might find me disgusting if I got too close. A big part of me believed no one would want to befriend someone like me. I didn't know then that it was shame that was making me think about myself this way, and I was letting it control my life.

Romantically, my past relationships could only be described as disastrous and disappointing. Some of them cheated on me, and some were even worse, for they ended up abusing me, taking advantage of me in some ways. It didn't matter that they were supposed to be someone I could rely on, people who were supposed to make me feel loved and enough.

Just like my uncle.

I thought no one would ever want someone with a story like mine, especially God. I even believed that anything I touched became too dirty, and I tried to take up the least amount of space or resources possible. Shame can do this to us. It is a tool of the enemy, designed to keep us from embracing the fullness of our identity in Christ.

We must not forget that Jesus came for the hurting and broken. Not for the polished. Not for the perfect.

For the wounded and the weary. For the ones hiding in shame, afraid they'll be seen and rejected.

Isaiah 61:7 says,

"Instead of your shame you will receive a double portion, and instead of disgrace you will rejoice in your inheritance."

God doesn't ignore our shame; He replaces it with something better.
He doesn't just forgive us; He restores what shame tried to steal from us.

To break free from shame, we have to understand that there's a difference between guilt, shame, and conviction. I didn't always know that.

Guilt says: "I did something bad."
Shame says: 'I am bad."

Conviction says: "I messed up, but I'm turning back to the truth."
Guilt can point you to grace.

Conviction can lead you to change. But shame? Shame wants to bury you in silence. Where conviction draws you close to God, shame pulls you away from Him.

For so long, I couldn't understand what they truly meant. I thought the weight of guilt and unworthiness was God's way of punishing me for my past. But it was a lie. God doesn't use shame to draw us to Him—He uses love and truth.

Romans 8:1 says,

Therefore, there is now no condemnation for those who are in Christ Jesus.

This verse changed everything. I saw myself from a new perspective—God's perspective. In Christ, I wasn't condemned. I wasn't defined by my past or my mistakes. I was forgiven. I was loved. And there was no room for shame in my new identity.

BREAKING THE POWER OF SHAME

Breaking free from shame was a process, especially since its grip on me was so tight. One of the biggest turning points in my journey came when I asked someone to pray for healing from my eating disorder and depression. He was one of the pastors in the church where I got baptized. And he did something that really helped me overcome shame. Instead of offering advice, he looked me in the eye and asked, "Why do you hate yourself?"

The question was so direct and hit me to the core. It echoed in my heart for a long time. I couldn't answer my pastor then, and for a while, I couldn't figure out an answer, but it opened a door I didn't know I had locked. His question led me to face the lies I had believed about myself. As I sought the answer, I started recognizing that I was using my pain to punish myself for things that weren't even my fault.

THE POWER OF TELLING THE TRUTH

Shame thrives in secrecy. As long as I kept my pain, my mistakes, and my trauma hidden, it had power over me. But the moment I began speaking the truth—to God, and to trusted people, and to others who had experienced similar things—shame began losing its grip.

James 5:16 says,

Confess your sins to each other and pray for each other so that you may be healed.

There's healing in confession—not just of sins, but of the lies we've believed and the pain we've hidden. Bringing these things to the light causes it to lose its power and the enemy can no longer use them to keep us bound. God designed us to be in fellowship with others, and confessing and praying for each other can lead to healing.

EMBRACING GOD'S FORGIVENESS

Another crucial step was learning to embrace God's forgiveness. I had spent so long trying to punish myself not just for my mistakes, but also for what people had done to me, falsely believing they were my mistakes as well. I believed it was my fault, and I thought I had to earn forgiveness.

But grace doesn't work like that.

Ephesians 2:8–9 says,

[8]For it is by grace you have been saved, through faith. And this is not your doing; it is the gift of God—[9]not by works, so that no one may boast.

God's forgiveness isn't something we can earn; it is a gift. And it's a gift offered freely, no matter how broken or worthless we feel.

I couldn't punish myself enough to make up for my past. All I could do was accept the gift of grace that Jesus offered me. In doing so, I began experiencing freedom from the shame that had weighed me down for so long.

Guilt is shame's close cousin. While shame says, "You are unworthy," guilt says, "What you've done is unforgivable." I carried both because of the things that I had done in response to my pain. I felt guilty for the way I had treated my body, for the relationships I had damaged, for the way I had hurt others and myself, and for the way I had misrepresented a powerful, loving God.

Guilt told me I didn't deserve a second chance. But just as God offers forgiveness for our sins, He also offers freedom from guilt. God had already forgiven me.

Psalm 103:12

As far as the east is from the west, so far has He removed our transgressions from us.

God doesn't hold our mistakes against us. When we come to Him in repentance, He forgives us completely and removes the stain of guilt from our lives. Knowing this, I knew it was time for me to forgive myself because if God can forgive me, who am I to condemn myself?

Galatians 5:1 says,

It is for freedom that Christ has set us free. Stand firm, then, and do not let yourselves be burdened again by a yoke of slavery.

Shame and guilt are forms of slavery. They keep us bound to our past and prevent us from stepping into the fullness of who God created us to be. But in Christ, we are free. Free from shame. Free from guilt. Free to live as the new creation we've been called to be.

REFLECTION: ESCAPING THE SHADOWS OF SHAME

RESPOND

1. What lie has shame made you believe about yourself? Do you still believe it?

2. Is there something you've kept hidden because you feared judgment or rejection?

3. What would it look like to receive God's forgiveness, not just intellectually, but emotionally and spiritually?

PRACTICING THE TRUTH

Escaping the shadows of shame and guilt is not easy, but as long as you stay in God's truth and be consistent in fighting the lies of the enemy, it is doable. I am a living proof of this.

Below are some guides to follow to free yourself from shame completely:

- **Name the Shame:** Write down the lie shame tells you. Then write the truth from God's Word next to it.

- **Confess to Heal:** Bring your pain to God in prayer, and when you're ready, share with a trusted friend, mentor, or counselor.

- **Speak Scripture Over Yourself:** Replace shame with promise. Say Isaiah 61:7 out loud.

- **Reject Isolation:** Don't let shame make you pull away. Stay connected to life-giving people.

- **Remember Jesus' Voice:** He doesn't shame you. He invites you into grace, truth, and healing.

JOURNAL PROMPT

Write a letter to the younger version of yourself—the one who felt ashamed, unworthy, or too far gone. Speak God's truth in your letter. Begin with this line:

"My beloved child, shame is not your name. You are not what happened to you. You are God's…"

PRAYER

Jesus,

I've spent too long believing the lies that shame told me. Lies that said I wasn't enough. Lies that said I'd never be clean. Today, I bring those lies to You and lay them down.

Thank You for forgiving me. Thank You for seeing me through eyes of love. Help me to walk in the freedom You've already given me—no more hiding. No more punishing myself. No more carrying what You already took to the cross.

Shame off me, Jesus. Truth in me. I am Yours.

In Jesus name,

Amen.

4

The Hard Work of Forgiveness – Healing Through Forgiveness with Boundaries

Forgiveness is a gift, not for them, but for myself.

When people talk about forgiveness, it often sounds simple, as if it's something you can just decide to do and instantly feel lighter. In reality, I learned that forgiveness is a deep, messy, and complicated process. For me, it wasn't just about letting go of the pain or pretending the hurt didn't exist. It was about releasing the grip that bitterness and resentment had over my life, and ultimately, learning how to protect my heart with healthy boundaries.

WHAT FORGIVENESS IS AND WHAT IT ISN'T

Before I could even consider forgiving those who had hurt me, I had to understand first what forgiveness really is. For a long time, I thought forgiving someone meant I was excusing their actions or saying that what they did to me was okay. I used to believe that in order to forgive, they first had to express that they were sorry. That misunderstanding kept me stuck in anger and resentment; the idea of excusing the people who abused me felt impossible.

However, I learned that forgiveness isn't about excusing the wrongs done to us. Forgiveness doesn't mean forgetting or acting like the pain never happened. It is about releasing the hold pain and bitterness have over our lives. It is about choosing not to let what others did to us define our future, even if they never apologize.

I had to learn that forgiveness doesn't require reconciliation. Just because I forgave someone didn't mean I had to invite them back into my life or trust them again. Forgiveness was my gift to myself—a way to set my heart free from the chains of bitterness. But for me to fully heal, the gift of forgiveness should come with boundaries, boundaries that allow me to protect myself from further harm.

FORGIVING MY ABUSERS

The first step in my journey toward forgiveness was the hardest part—facing my abusers. From my uncle who molested me for years, to the boys who assaulted me, and to the man who raped me, the idea of forgiving them felt unimaginable. How could I forgive the ones who had stolen so much from me? How could I let go of the pain when it still felt like a part of who I was?

Who was I without the pain? Without the anger and bitterness?

But I realized that forgiving them wasn't for their benefit—it was for mine. Holding onto bitterness and anger only kept me in a prison of pain. It was allowing their actions to have continued control over my life, even years after the abuse had ended. I was tired of carrying that weight. I was tired of letting them still have power over me.

Forgiving them wasn't an act of excusing what they did. It was an act of releasing the hold their actions had on my heart. It was me saying, *"You don't get to control my life anymore."* And as hard as it was to let go, each step toward forgiveness brought a little more freedom. The chains of anger and resentment began to loosen, and I started to see that the forgiveness wasn't for them—it was for me. It was for my healing.

FORGIVING MYSELF

While forgiving my abusers was a difficult process, I didn't expect that one of the hardest people to forgive was myself.

I had carried so much guilt and shame for the choices I made during those years of trauma. I felt guilty for the ways I had harmed myself, the people I had hurt, and the destructive behaviors I had used to cope. I even blamed myself for the abuse and somehow convinced myself it was my fault.

Even though I knew God had forgiven me, I struggled to extend that same forgiveness to myself. For years, I held myself to an impossible standard of perfection, punishing myself for my perceived failures. But just like forgiving others, forgiving myself was an act of releasing the hold that shame had over me. It was about letting go of the guilt I carried and allowing myself to heal from the inside out. I had to remind myself that if God could forgive me, then I had no right to hold that guilt against myself.

If I held it any longer, it was like saying the price Jesus paid to set me free wasn't enough. But it was more than enough. His sacrifice was not for nothing. It was time I believed this truth.

SETTING HEALTHY BOUNDARIES

As I began to walk in forgiveness, I realized the importance of boundaries. Forgiving someone didn't mean I had to allow them back into my life or expose myself to further harm. In fact, part of my healing journey was learning how to set boundaries to protect my heart and my mental and emotional well-being.

Boundaries were essential in my relationship with my abusers. I had to accept that forgiving them didn't mean I had to have a relationship with them. I could forgive them in my heart without ever wanting to see them again. Setting boundaries was about creating space where I could heal and grow without allowing toxic influences to pull me back into the old patterns of pain.

Jesus Himself demonstrated the importance of boundaries. He forgave those who persecuted Him, but He also set boundaries in relationships, choosing when to engage and when to withdraw. He showed that love and forgiveness don't mean sacrificing your well-being or allowing others to keep harming you.

Ephesians 4:32 says,

Be kind and compassionate to one another, forgiving each other, just as in Christ God forgave you.

But forgiving someone doesn't mean giving them unlimited access to your life. Boundaries are an act of love—both for yourself and for the person you are forgiving. By setting boundaries, it doesn't give your abusers any more chance to harm you in any way. Boundaries allow space for healing and protect your heart from further harm.

UNDERSTANDING BOUNDARIES THROUGH A BIBLICAL LENS

Boundaries aren't about building walls; they're about building wisdom. They protect what's sacred—your heart, your peace, and your healing process. Setting boundaries doesn't mean you're bitter or unforgiving. It means you're aware of what you need in order to heal and grow.

For a long time, I thought boundaries were harsh or unloving. But Jesus Himself set boundaries. He walked away from crowds. He retreated to quiet places. He didn't give everyone the same access to His time, His heart, or His presence. And He never apologized for it.

Boundaries say:

- You don't get to speak to me like that.
- I forgive you, but I'm choosing not to re-enter that relationship.
- I can love you and still say no.
- I'm not responsible for your response—only for my obedience to God.

Some people won't understand your boundaries. That's okay. You're not responsible for managing their expectations—you're responsible for protecting the healing God is doing in your life.

You can forgive someone fully and still never let them close again. That's not hate. That's wisdom.

THE FREEDOM OF FORGIVENESS

Walking through the hard work of forgiveness, allowed me to experience a freedom that I had never known before. The weight of unforgiveness lifted, and I found myself able to breathe again. Forgiveness didn't erase the pain of what had happened, but it gave me the freedom to move forward, breaking the chains of the past.

The actions of others no longer defined me. I was no longer imprisoned by the hurt or controlled by the memories of abuse. Forgiveness allowed me to step into the fullness of my identity in Christ.

Colossians 3:13 says,

Bear with each other and forgive one another if any of you has a grievance against someone. Forgive as the Lord forgave you.

Forgiveness is an act of obedience to God, but it's also an act of love for ourselves. When we forgive, we release ourselves from the prison of resentment and step into the freedom Christ offers us.

REFLECTION: FORGIVING WITH BOUNDARIES

RESPOND

1. Is there someone you need to forgive—not for their sake, but for your own freedom?

2. Have you confused forgiveness with reconciliation, thinking that one requires the other?

3. Are there boundaries you need to set to protect your heart as you heal?

PRACTICING THE TRUTH

Forgiveness is a process. It doesn't happen all at once. But with the following steps, you can move closer to freedom:

1. Take a moment to reflect on the areas in your life where unforgiveness might still be holding you captive.

2. Write down the names of those you're still holding resentment toward—including yourself.

3. Ask God to begin softening your heart, helping you release the weight of unforgiveness.

4. Finally, ask God for wisdom and courage to set boundaries where needed, knowing that forgiveness doesn't mean allowing repeated harm.

JOURNAL PROMPT

Write a letter to the person—or people—you need to forgive, including yourself. You don't need to give it to them. This is for you and God. Let your heart speak honestly.

Then, at the bottom of your letter, write these words:

"I release you. You don't get to control my heart, my mind, or my future anymore.
I choose forgiveness—not because you deserve it, but because Jesus forgave me, and I want to be free."

If it's yourself you're forgiving, write:

"I release myself. I no longer carry what Jesus already paid for. I choose to forgive myself because He already has."

PRAYER

Father,

Thank You for the gift of forgiveness. You saw all the pain, all the wounds, and all the people who hurt me, and still, You offered freedom. Thank You that I don't have to carry bitterness or resentment. Help me forgive not because it's easy, but because it's what leads to healing.

Give me the strength to release those I've been holding in my heart. Help me set healthy boundaries so that I can heal in peace and not repeat old cycles. Show me how to forgive others, how to forgive myself, and how to walk in the freedom You died to give me.

I trust You with the process, even when it's slow. Even when it hurts. I know that You are working healing deep within me.

In Jesus' name,

Amen.

5

Trusting God as Healer and Protector: Wrestling with Faith, Disappointment, and the Nearness of God

He was there through every moment of it, even when I couldn't feel His presence.

There were so many times in my life when I questioned where God was. I wondered how a loving and protective God could have allowed the things that happened to me—the abuse, the trauma, the self-destructive behaviors. I felt abandoned by Him, left to navigate my pain alone. For a long time, I believed that God wasn't there. But looking back, I can now see that He was always with me, even when I couldn't feel Him. He was protecting me in ways I didn't yet understand, working quietly in the background to prepare me for healing.

WHERE WAS GOD IN MY PAIN?

When we're going through deep suffering, we question everything.

Why is this happening to me?

Why is it so hard?

Why me?

Do I deserve this?

But one of the hardest questions we face when we're going through deep suffering is this one: Where is God in my pain?

It's easy to believe that God might not love us, because if He truly loved us, He would have stopped the pain before it happened. But we often forget that we live in a broken world, where sin and suffering are part of life.

The abuse I endured wasn't from God, and it wasn't His will for my life. Yet, He was there through every moment of it, even when I couldn't feel His presence.

I realized the importance of prayer in our journey towards healing. Prayer was my way of communicating with God, even when I couldn't feel Him. Over time, I learned how to pray in a new way. I started creating a space to sit with God in the stillness and ask Him specific questions about the painful moments in my life.

"Where were You when this happened?"

"Why did You allow this?"

"What were You doing during that time?"

I had been too afraid to ask these questions before, unsure whether I would hear an answer, or if I even wanted to know the truth.

Trusting God doesn't always come easily, especially when we've been wounded. But just because we struggle to trust doesn't mean we are alone in the journey. Sometimes, trust isn't something we start with—it's something we borrow.

We borrow it from others who've walked with God longer, those who have seen His faithfulness firsthand. When we're in the midst of a struggle, it's often hard to trust God. It's hard to stay still and let God, and it feels like our faith is not enough. When this happens, I rely on people around me—my husband, my mentors and teachers, and my brothers and sisters in Christ. I remember the stories they've told, stories about when they had trusted God, and He showed up. Their stories of faith give me faith and confidence to trust in God as well.

We borrow trust from Scripture, from the disciples, the prophets, and even from the psalmist who cried out in despair but still proclaimed:

Psalm 13:5 says,

But I trust in your unfailing love…

When our own faith feels weak, we can lean on the faith of others and let their testimonies remind us of who God is. And eventually, as we walk with Him, trust moves from something we borrow and becomes something we own.

LEARNING TO HEAR GOD'S VOICE

I learned to listen. But it wasn't easy; I had help. It was only with the help with the Holy Spirit that I learned how to listen to God.

In moments of quiet prayer, God revealed how He had been with me all along. He showed me the ways He had protected my heart, how He had kept me from complete destruction, and how His presence had never left me, even when I felt most alone.

It wasn't an immediate process. First, I had to recognize that the noises in my head were just that—noises. They didn't do me any good, but I knew there was one sound I needed to hear—God's voice.

I had to practice quieting my thoughts, fears, and inner noise and truly tune into God's voice through the Holy Spirit. As I listened, He began showing me His faithfulness, even in the darkest look times. I realized, while God hadn't stopped the abuse from happening, He had been there protecting me in ways I couldn't see at the time. He had shielded my soul from being completely crushed. And He had a plan to heal me.

Isaiah 41:10 became a source of hope and strength during that season:

"So do not fear, for I am with you; do not be dismayed, for I am your God. I will strengthen you and help you; I will uphold you with my righteous right hand."

Even when I couldn't see Him, God was holding me up, strengthening me, and keeping me from being completely destroyed.

GOD AS PROTECTOR

It took me a long time to understand that God's protection doesn't always mean we'll be shielded from every painful experience. Instead, His protection often comes in ways we don't expect. He protects our hearts, our souls, and our eternal destiny.

The enemy wanted to use the trauma I endured to destroy me completely—to convince me I was worthless, and that life wasn't worth living. But God's protection kept me from going down that path. His hand was there, even when I was contemplating ending my life. He pulled me back from the edge.

I began to understand that God wasn't distant; He was my constant protector working behind the scenes. He revealed specific moments in my life where His protection had been present. Whether it was a situation He removed me from, or a truth He whispered into my heart when the lies overwhelmed me. His protection was also visible in the people He placed in my life, such as my mom. When I was ready to give up, my mother's words—The devil is a liar— were God's way of reminding me that the lies I believed were not from Him.

Though difficult situations did occur, He didn't allow them to consume me. He protected the core of who I was, even when I didn't realize it. And more than that, He had a plan set in motion to heal me from the inside out.

GOD AS HEALER

Healing didn't begin when the abuse ended. It began when I finally surrendered my pain to God and allowed Him to do the deep work of restoring my heart. I had spent years trying to heal on my own through unhealthy coping, self-destructive habits, and striving for perfection. But real healing came when I finally brought my brokenness to God.

Psalm 147:3 says,

He heals the brokenhearted and binds up their wounds.

God didn't just patch up the surface-level wounds—He went deep. He healed the parts of me that had been shattered by trauma and pain. It wasn't instant. It was a process—one I'm still walking through. But He has been faithful every step of the way.

When I look back now, I can see how God was healing me through the people He placed in my life—friends, family members, counselors—and especially through His Word and presence, which became more real to me as I surrendered more and more to Him.

HEALING THE DEEPER WOUNDS

The wounds that took the longest to heal weren't physical. They were the ones that shaped my identity—lies that said I was worthless, unlovable, and broken beyond repair. But God didn't just want to heal the pain; He wanted to restore my identity by making me see the truth of who I am.

For a long time, I thought my life would just be a constant cycle of survival, relapses, and suffering. When I was going through hospitalization programs for my eating disorder, I considered myself a "lifer." It was a title I heard passed around in those therapy sessions with other people. Healing seemed impossible, and there was no way out.

But God had more for me.

God wanted me to experience true freedom. It is the only kind of freedom that comes when we allow Him to heal the deepest parts of our heart.

I had to face the lies I had believed for years and let God speak truth into them:

> *You are Mine. You are made in My image. You are worthy of My love.*

THE ONGOING JOURNEY OF HEALING

Healing is not a one-time event, and surrendering to the healing process is the first step. But it doesn't stop there, because healing is a lifelong process of surrender.

I had to let go of my need to control it. I had to believe that I didn't have to do it alone. I had to push past the fear of looking back and digging deep, no matter how overwhelming it was. And every time I brought my pain to God, He met me with grace.

Philippians 1:6 says,

Being confident of this, that He who began a good work in you will carry it on to completion until the day of Christ Jesus.

Although, even now, there are days when old wounds feel tender. But I've learned that those moments aren't proof that healing hasn't worked. They are invitations to keep walking with God and trusting Him to heal the areas that still hurt. I've learned that the more I bring it all to Him, the easier and quicker it gets to get through the hard times.

Healing is a journey, and God is patient.

He never asks us to walk through it alone.

He walks with us, protects us from lies, and gently guides us into truth.

God isn't done with me yet, and He's not done with you either.

The healing may take time, but God is faithful to finish what He starts.

REFLECTION: TRUSTING GOD AS HEALER AND PROTECTOR

RESPOND

First, ask yourself:

1. In what areas of my life do I still need healing?
2. Where have I been holding on to pain, afraid to trust God with the deeper wounds of my heart?

Then, ask God:

1. Where were You during that pain?
2. How have You protected me when I didn't see it?
3. What are You still healing in me?

Write it down. Listen for His voice. He is present in every step.

JOURNAL PROMPT

Before you begin writing, speak this truth out loud:

"God has always been with me. Even when I couldn't see Him, He was protecting and healing me."

Now take a moment to write a letter to God, sharing the areas where you've struggled to trust Him. Be honest about your questions, your pain, and your fears. Then, ask Him to show you where He has been with you all along.

Let your words be raw and real. This is not about saying the "right" thing. It's about inviting Him into the deepest places of your heart and giving Him permission to heal you.

PRAYER

Father,

Thank You for being my Protector and Healer. Even when I couldn't see You, You were with me. Even when I questioned You, You were working. Help me trust You with the areas of my heart that still hurt. I surrender my pain to You. Lead me step by step into healing.

Thank You for shielding me from destruction, for speaking truth into my life, and for being patient with me in the process. I trust You to finish the good work You have begun in me.

In Jesus' name,

Amen.

6

Redeemed and Repurposed – Finding Purpose in the Ashes

Out of the ashes comes something beautiful.

There was a time in my life when I truly believed I was unwanted, and I wondered what was the purpose of my pain? Why did I have to hurt? I didn't understand why God allowed my pain. It felt like the suffering I had endured, the trauma I carried, and the scars I bore were too deep, too permanent. What good could possibly come out of it? I felt like the leftovers—too broken, too much, or maybe just not enough. Rejection had left its mark on me, convincing me that I didn't belong, that I didn't have a place, and that no one would ever choose me. I carried those wounds into every space I entered—relationships, ministry, and even moments alone with God. I wondered if He could really use someone like me.

I couldn't imagine how God could take something so broken and make something worthwhile out of it. But as I began to heal and lean into the truth of who I was in Christ, I discovered something powerful: God has a way of taking the ashes of our deepest pain and turning them into something beautiful. He redeems our suffering, giving it meaning far beyond what we could ever imagine.

God doesn't wait until we feel worthy to call us. He doesn't need us to be spotless to set us apart. He calls us while we're still hurting. He invites us while we're still unsure. And when He calls us, He doesn't change His mind.

NOT REJECTED

Rejection tries to define us by the voices that walked away, the people who didn't choose us, or the rooms we were never invited into. It doesn't just wound us; it shapes how we see ourselves. It's not always the big moments that scar us; it's the accumulation of smaller ones. Not being picked, being excluded, being forgotten. Over time, these moments start to echo louder than the truth.

I questioned if I was truly loved by God or just tolerated. I thought I was bothering Him if I asked for things in prayer. I worried that I prayed too much. I wondered if maybe His promises were for others, but not for someone like me. The enemy used rejection like a lens, distorting my ability to receive love and making me believe that I had to prove my worth to everyone, even to God.

But God's voice is different.

He doesn't base His love on how others have treated us. His love doesn't waver with our wounds. God sees us fully, and still calls us chosen. He sees every moment we've been overlooked, and He steps in and says, "I see you. I choose you."

Isaiah 43:1 says,

Do not fear, for I have redeemed you; I have summoned you by name; you are mine.

There is something profoundly healing in those last three words: You are mine. God's redemption doesn't just rescue us—it reclaims the parts of our story that we thought disqualified us. It doesn't matter who walked away, who said we weren't good enough, or how many times we've been overlooked—God's love silences those lies.

He doesn't just tolerate us—He calls us by name. That's personal. That's intentional. That's love.

THE PROMISE OF REDEMPTION

For years, I struggled to believe that anything good could come from the suffering I had endured. I didn't see how my story could possibly fit into God's purpose for my life. But as I lean into God's Word, I learned that He uses everything we've been through—both good and bad—not only to reveal His love for us but for His plans in our lives to come to pass.

Romans 8:28 says,

And we know that in all things God works for the good of those who love Him, who have been called according to His purpose.

This is one of the most powerful verses that became a foundation in my healing journey.

God's promise in this verse doesn't say that everything that happens to us is good; it says that God works all things together for the good. Even the darkest moments of our lives, even the things that were meant to destroy us—God can use them for His purpose and glory. That doesn't mean the pain is diminished or it was part of His will for us. It simply means that nothing is wasted in God's hands.

BEAUTY FROM ASHES

How can beauty come out of ashes? But God loves us so much and cares about us that He won't let us stay in ruin. He won't leave us in mourning because of what we've been through.

Isaiah 61:3 speaks of God's promise to *"bestow on them a crown of beauty instead of ashes, the oil of joy instead of mourning, and a garment of praise instead of a spirit of despair."* When I first read this verse, I was still at the beginning of my healing process. I couldn't yet see how beauty could rise from the ashes of my trauma, but this promise gave me hope. It was a reminder that God's intention for me was not to leave me broken, but to restore and redeem me completely.

As I healed, another verse, Mark 5:41, became deeply personal to me. In this verse, Jesus says to a dead girl, *"Talitha Koum,"* which means, *"Little girl, I say to you, get up!"* I felt like God was calling me out of the death I had lived in for so long, calling me to rise from the ashes of my trauma and the death that was waiting for me if I kept living the way I did. I was destroying myself with my eating disorder. God was calling me to step into the new life He had for me.

It wasn't just the call to life that moved me but also what Jesus did next. After raising the girl, He told the people to give her something to eat. That small detail resonated deeply with me, especially because of my battle with anorexia. It felt like God was not only calling me to life but also saying, "Now, let me feed you." He was offering me the bread of life—the spiritual nourishment I so desperately needed.

For years, I had starved myself, not just physically but also spiritually. I was empty, trying to survive on my own strength, disconnected from the true source of life. Trying to get through the day with just scraps. When God called me from death, He didn't just want to bring me back to life—He wanted me to be nourished with His word, His truth, His love. To restore not just my body, but my soul.

FINDING PURPOSE IN PAIN

Another remarkable transformation I went through as I healed was the shift in my desires. Before, my focus had been on survival. My goal was to get through each day without being overwhelmed by the weight of my pain or my constant need for control and distractions from it. My ambitions were centered on myself, on building a life that could mask the hurt I carried and avoid being around people. My routines were consumed with habits of movement, like walks and workouts, and things I could do to avoid food and social situations. I even pursued a career in wildlife biology, hoping I never have to be around other people. I could just escape into the wild. I never stopped to consider others or how my actions affected those around me.

But as I came to embrace my true identity in Christ, my desires began to shift. God planted new dreams in my heart, centered not on my own success, but on helping others find the same freedom I had found. The deeper I went into my healing journey, the more I realized that my life wasn't just about me.

God had a bigger plan.

God wanted to use my story to bring hope and healing to others who were walking through their own valleys. He wanted to take my pain and turn it into a source of encouragement for those who felt hopeless. I realized He didn't save me just for myself, and my pain wasn't just something to survive; He saved me to share hope with others, and He could use my story for His glory.

GOD'S REDEEMING PURPOSE

As I continued to heal and share my story, I saw firsthand how God redeemed my pain. Every conversation I had with someone who felt lost in their trauma, every opportunity I had to speak about the freedom I found in Christ, became a reminder of God's incredible power to bring good out of what was meant for harm.

Revelation 12:11 says,

They triumphed over him by the blood of the Lamb and by the word of their testimony.

There is power in sharing our testimony. Our testimony is our story. It not only strengthens our faith, but it also helps others see the hope and freedom that is available in Christ. Our story has the power to break chains in someone else's life.

There's something incredibly freeing about knowing that our pain is not without purpose. When we understand that God can use every part of our story, even the darkest moments, for His kingdom, it changes the way we see ourselves. We are no longer victims of our circumstances but redeemed children of God, walking in His purpose, and carrying the message of hope to others.

STEPPING INTO A LIFE OF PURPOSE

Walking in purpose means allowing God to use every part of our lives—the good and the bad—to fulfill His will. For me, it meant embracing the calling to help others who were still trapped in the same darkness I had once known. It meant being vulnerable enough to share my journey, knowing my story wasn't just for me, but also for others who needed to hear it. My life is not just for me anymore.

The more I leaned into God's purpose for my life, the more I saw the beauty He was creating from the ashes. My story wasn't about shame anymore; it was about redemption. My identity wasn't defined by my trauma; it was defined by God's love and grace. My life wasn't just about my healing; it was about being a light to those who were still in darkness. Your survival is evidence that God still has a plan for you.

Ephesians 2:10 says,

For we are God's handiwork, created in Christ Jesus to do good works, which God prepared in advance for us to do.

This verse became a guiding truth for me as I walked into my purpose. I realized, God had created me for more than just surviving my pain. He had prepared good works for me to do, works that would bring others into the healing and freedom I had found in Him.

The enemy tried to destroy you, but God has the final word.
Redeemed.
Chosen.
Called.

I didn't think someone like me could ever be trusted with a calling, but God showed me how wrong I was. Purpose isn't just for people who seem to have it all together. We were all created with purpose. It's part of our identity. And the pain we try to run from can be the place He calls us to speak from.

My story isn't perfect, but it's real. Real stories change lives. God doesn't need you to be polished and perfect; He just needs you to be surrendered.

REFLECTION: REDEEMED FOR A REASON

RESPOND

1. What have you gone through that could encourage someone else? Take a moment to think about how God might want to use your story. Reflect on areas that once made you feel unwanted or disqualified.

2. Where have you seen God redeem something painful and use it for good? Write down moments in your life where God met you in the ashes and created something beautiful.

Ask God to show you how He wants to use your healing journey for His glory. You are not disqualified because of your past. You are called. And your story—every part of it—can be a testimony of His redeeming love.

JOURNAL PROMPT

Take some time to write your testimony based on the following questions:

1. What has God redeemed you from?
2. What pain or trauma has He healed or still healing?
3. How has your life changed since you surrender to Him?

If writing your story feels too hard right now, start by answering this:

Where do I feel most disqualified—and what might God want to do with that place?

121

PRAYER

Father,

Thank You for redeeming what was broken and using it for good. Thank You for not letting my pain go to waste. I give You every part of my story—the good, the hard, the ugly—and I ask You to use it for Your glory. Plant new dreams in my heart. Show me how to walk in the purpose You've prepared for me. Help me see myself not as a victim, but as a vessel of Your grace and healing. Let my story be a light to others who need to know that there is still hope.

In Jesus' name,

Amen.

7

The Battle for the Word – Fighting for the Kingdom, Not Just for Ourselves

For we are soldiers at war, and we have a kingdom to fight for.

There's a battle most people don't talk about, and when they do, it's often misunderstood. As Christians, we are always at war. We are at war for our mind, our calling, our freedom, but ultimately, it's not just about us.

It's not just about you; it's also about the Kingdom. It's about what God has placed inside you to impact the world, which is what the enemy is after. If he can't destroy you, he'll try to distract you. If he can't take your faith, he'll try to twist it. If he can't stop your healing, he'll try to convince you it's only for you, that it has no deeper purpose.

This is why the battle for the Kingdom of God is often misunderstood. The enemy convinces us that our pain and suffering, our healing and redemption, are only for us. But God has bigger plans for each of us, and we are parts of something bigger than ourselves. This is where the battle for the Word comes in. The Word of God must be deeply rooted in us, because it is our weapon to win the war we are in.

THE ENEMY

Jesus told a parable in Mark 4 that changed my perception about the Word of God. He said the Word is like a seed sown into hearts. Some falls on rocky ground, some among thorns, and some on good soil. But there's a line in verse 15 that always stands out to me:

Mark 4:15 says,

…As soon as they hear it, Satan comes and takes away the word that was sown in them.

Satan comes immediately to steal the Word that was sown. He didn't waste any time, not giving the Word a chance to take root within you. That's the enemy's strategy. He's after the Word. Not just your peace. Not just your healing. The seed—the truth, the assignment, the message—that God placed inside of you.

The enemy isn't afraid of your recovery—he's afraid of your testimony. He's afraid of you getting back up with purpose. He's worried that your healing will multiply into other people's freedom. So what does he do? He attacks your mind. He twists the truth. He plants fear. He stirs comparison, discouragement, distraction—anything to keep you self-focused instead of Kingdom-focused.

The enemy doesn't mind if you go to church, as long as you don't "become" the Church. He doesn't mind if you read the Bible, as long as you don't "live" it. He doesn't mind if you heal, as long as you stay quiet about it. But the moment you rise up and say, "I'm not just free—I'm fighting for the Kingdom," the battle intensifies.

For years, I didn't recognize the spiritual dimension of my struggles. I thought the feelings of worthlessness, shame, and fear were just a part of who I was—an inevitable outcome of what had happened to me. As I drew closer to God and learned to hear His voice, He revealed that these battles were not attacks from within me, but rather from something much bigger than the visible world around me. The enemy's lies had been keeping me bound in shame, self-hatred, and fear, trying to get me to destroy myself, an image bearer of Christ.

After I attempted to take my own life and began following Jesus, my dad gave me a book called *Prescription for Worry* by James P. Gills. He said it was probably the best gift he'd ever given me. My dad wasn't loud about his faith, but he knew the power of the Word of God. I remember moments when he'd gently ask, "Have you brought that to the Lord yet?" always pointing me back to prayer.

I read that book twice, and it was one of the first things that helped shift my perspective. It helped me recognize that my anxiety wasn't just emotional; it was also spiritual. That gift marked the beginning of my healing journey, and I'll always be grateful. My dad has since passed away, and I miss him deeply. But I hold on to those moments, knowing he planted seeds of faith in my life when I needed them most.

SPIRITUAL WARFARE

Spiritual warfare is real. It's not just a metaphor or a dramatic idea, but a daily reality. It is real even as you read this book.

Ephesians 6:12 says,

Our struggle is not against flesh and blood, but against rulers, authorities, powers of this dark world, and spiritual forces of evil in the heavenly realms.

It is crucial that we acknowledge we're at war, because if we don't know it, we won't fight. We'll live passive lives, thinking our thoughts are just moods and our confusion is just personality. Many of those battles are spiritual attacks against the seed of God in our life.

The war is for your mind. Why? Because what you believe shapes how you live. If the enemy can corrupt your thoughts, he can delay your calling. If he can isolate you in shame, he can keep your testimony silent. If he can twist your identity, he can keep you from walking in authority.

Once I saw the battle for what it was, I realized I didn't have to fight alone.

SPIRITUAL ARMOR

Here's the truth: you've been given armor. You are not defenseless. God loves you so much to send you without help into battle. **Ephesians 6** lays it out clearly for us. Each piece of this armor represents something we need to fight against Satan.

- **The belt of truth (v.14)** so you can identify the lies. This is the foundation. It's what everything else hangs on. Putting on the belt of truth means rejecting the lies that try to define you. It means starting your day by anchoring your identity in what God says, not what your feelings scream. When the enemy tries to convince me I'm worthless or dirty and not good enough, I hold on to the truth of God's Word, knowing that I'm fearfully and wonderfully made, loved, and redeemed.

- **The breastplate of righteousness (v.14)** to protect your heart. When you know you're made righteous through Christ—not through performance—you don't live in shame or striving. Righteousness means walking in obedience, but it also means resting in who you are because of Jesus. The Word teaches us that out of the abundance of the heart; the mouth speaks. What are you speaking over yourself? What are you allowing others to speak over you? What internal and external pressures are you allowing to dictate your life? Let it be a reflection of God's truth by guarding your heart.

- **The shoes of peace (v.15)** to help you stand firm. Peace is not passive. It is power. You walk in peace when you remember who goes before you. When your soul is anchored in God, the chaos of life won't knock you down so easily. In moments of chaos or fear, I could rest in the peace that comes from knowing Christ and the security I have in Him.

- **The shield of faith (v.16)** to extinguish the flaming arrows. This is your defense against the fiery darts—lies, fear, anxiety, temptation. You lift your shield every time you say, "I believe God more than I believe this attack." Even a mustard seed of faith can block a storm of doubt. Faith reminds me that even when I cannot see or understand what God is doing, I can trust Him.

- **The helmet of salvation (v.17)** to guard your mind. The enemy wants your mind. He'll whisper confusion, insecurity, distraction, and every lie he can come up with. But when you put on the helmet of salvation, you protect your thoughts with the truth that you belong to Jesus. You're saved. You're secure. You're sealed. Most of our battles are within our minds, but the mind is like a two-way road.

Things come in (what we hear, see, read, etc.) and things go out (our own thoughts and meditations). Let me ask you this: if we wouldn't knowingly consume something unclean physically, why would we allow impure or destructive things into our hearts and minds?

- **The sword of the Spirit (v.17)**, which is the Word of God—your weapon. When we think of an actual sword and going to battle, we probably won't be very successful on the battlefield if we have no training or experience with swords. We have to know how to use one, even familiarize ourselves with its weight. We must train our bodies, align our moves with the sword, as though we're performing a beautiful dance. This same principle applies to the Word. If you have no experience with it, haven't taken the time to learn it, work with it, and let it become a part of you, you're stepping onto the battlefield unprepared. Remember, you don't fight thoughts with more thoughts; you fight lies with Scripture. Speak it. Declare it. Wield it. Jesus used the Word to silence the enemy, and so can you.

PRAYER

Prayer is our second weapon of attack. It is the last piece of our armor, which is often forgotten and overlooked.

In my journey to healing, one of the most important lessons I've learned was how to pray in the Spirit and with authority. My prayers were no longer just requests or desperate pleas for help; they became declarations of God's truth. I began praying scriptures over myself, declaring the promises of God over my life and the lives of those around me. The more I prayed in the Spirit and in alignment with God's Word, the more I felt His power at work in my life.

Prayer is the most powerful force we can release into the atmosphere around us. It invites heaven into our situation. When we couple it with praise, which is a heart postured in gratitude and admiration for God, we truly let God take His throne over our circumstances.

You don't need to feel strong to fight; you just need to be equipped. The more I tried to fight in my own strength, the more exhausted I became. But when I fought from a place of rest in God's authority, I discovered the strength was never mine to muster—it was His to supply.

WHAT WE'RE FIGHTING FOR

There is something powerful about realizing the fight is bigger than you. That it's not just about your survival—it's about souls. It's about the people on the other side of your obedience. Their freedom is connected to your willingness to stand firm.

When we fight spiritual battles, we're not fighting for victory—we're fighting from it. Jesus already won.

Our job is to stand.

To guard the Word.

To stay awake.

To hold the line when it would be easier to retreat.

When you feel overwhelmed, remember this: The same power that raised Jesus from the dead lives in you. You don't fight alone; you fight with heaven backing you.

This isn't just about healing anymore, but also reclaiming territory. It's about rising up not just as survivors, but as soldiers, clothed in truth, armed with faith, and carrying the sword of the Spirit, praying always.

You were made for more than survival. You were made for war. And your victory advances the Kingdom.

GUARDING THE SEED – THE BATTLE BENEATH THE SURFACE

In Mark 4, Jesus explains why the Word doesn't always produce fruit. It's not because the seed is faulty; it's because the soil is under attack. The moment God speaks, the enemy tries to steal it. That's why spiritual warfare often increases right after a breakthrough. You hear a Word, you receive a promise, you begin to believe again, and suddenly you feel attacked. That's not a coincidence; that's war.

The rocky soil? That's when we receive the Word with joy but don't let it take root. The thorns? That's when distractions, anxiety, or comparison choke it out. The enemy doesn't care how; he just wants the seed dead.

But when we guard our soil, water the Word, stay rooted in community, and keep returning to God, we become good soil. The Word grows in us and multiply through us—thirty, sixty, a hundred times what was sown.

YOU'RE NOT JUST FIGHTING FOR YOURSELF

You are not the only one affected by your healing. There are people on the other side of your freedom. Your children. Your future spouse. The people you're called to reach and teach. The people who will hear your story and find hope. The enemy knows that if you rise, others rise with you. That's why he attacks so hard.

But here's the thing: you're not just being attacked—you're being trusted. God trusted you with this battle because He intends to use your victory for others. You're not just recovering. You're reclaiming. And the territory you fight for now is going to bless generations.

FROM SURVIVAL TO KINGDOM ASSIGNMENT

The enemy wants you stuck in survival mode—just making it through each day. But God is calling you to a mission. The battle isn't over just because you found healing. Your healing was just the beginning. Now you're called to advance, to fight for others, and to build the Kingdom.

Matthew 28:19-20 says,

[19]Therefore go and make disciples of all nations, baptizing them in the name of the Father and of the Son and of the Holy Spirit, [20]and teaching them to obey everything I have commanded you. And surely, I am with you always, to the very end of the age.

You were never just fighting for peace—you were fighting for purpose. And you weren't just called to heal—you were called to lead.

YOUR BATTLE PLAN

Spiritual warfare isn't something we face only in crisis—it's a daily reality for every believer. The good news is, you are not fighting for victory; you are fighting *from* victory. Jesus has already overcome the enemy, and your job is to stand in the truth of what He's done.

Take a moment now to examine your life.

1. Where has the enemy been whispering lies?

2. Have you been fighting in your own strength, or have you been leaning on the truth of God's Word?

3. Are you wearing the armor, or have you laid some of it down?

4. Are you asking God what He says about the battle you're in?

Remember:

- The belt of truth reminds you of who you are.
- The breastplate of righteousness protects your heart.
- The gospel of peace anchors you in chaos.
- The shield of faith extinguishes every lie.
- The helmet of salvation guards your thoughts.

- The sword of the Spirit and prayer are your weapons.

Use the armor and weapons that God had provided to aid you in this war. You were made for victory. You were made to stand. So take your place, warrior. The King has equipped you to fight not just for yourself, but for the Kingdom.

REFLECTION: WHAT ARE YOU REALLY FIGHTING FOR?

RESPOND

1. What lies has the enemy tried to sow in your mind to steal the Word God planted?

2. Have you ever mistaken a spiritual attack for personal failure? If so, how did you handle it?

3. How can you begin to shift from a survival mindset to a Kingdom mission mindset?

4. Who might be on the other side of your freedom—someone who needs your testimony?

5. Think about the armor of God—are there pieces you've been leaving behind? Are you fighting from a place of victory or exhaustion?

6. Have I made room for God's Word to become my weapon?

JOURNAL PROMPT

God has planted something in you. What is one thing He's been speaking to your heart lately through His Word, prayer, or even this book?

Write it down like a seed you're choosing to protect.

Now ask: What has tried to steal or choke that Word? Name it. Then write a short prayer asking God to help you guard that seed and grow it into Kingdom impact.

PRAYER

Father,

Thank You for opening my eyes to the battle I've been living in. I don't want to live unaware or unarmed. Today, I choose to put on the full armor of God.

Belt of truth—fasten it around me.
Breastplate of righteousness—guard my heart.
Shoes of peace—steady my steps.
Shield of faith—extinguish every lie.
Helmet of salvation—protect my mind.
Sword of the Spirit—train me to use Your Word.

I'm not just fighting for myself. I'm fighting for others. Let my obedience make a way for someone else's breakthrough. I declare that I am not a victim—I am a soldier in Your army, and I stand on the victory Jesus already won.

In Jesus' name,

Amen.

8

Surrender Isn't Weakness— Letting Go of Control and Running to God

Control makes you feel strong, but surrender makes you whole.

The battle we face isn't always loud. Sometimes it's silent, buried under habits we've labeled "normal." After learning to stand and fight, I had to face something more subtle but just as powerful—the fight to let go. In this stage of my journey, I didn't need more armor; I needed open hands.

For years, I thought control was the only thing keeping me safe.

Controlling my food.
Controlling my schedule.
Controlling my emotions.
Controlling who got close.

I didn't call it fear—I called it "discipline." I didn't call it an addiction—I called it "motivation." The truth is, I was terrified. I didn't want to fall apart again. I didn't want to be vulnerable. And I definitely didn't want to feel powerless.

So I clung to control like it was a life raft. But it wasn't saving me; it was drowning me.

THE ILLUSION OF CONTROL

Recently, I read a book called *The Genesis Process* by Michael Dye. The book talks about how we don't do things for no reason; we do them because, at some point, they worked.

Controlling my body made me feel like I had power when everything else felt chaotic. The obsession with food gave me something to focus on, so I didn't have to feel. The routines made me feel safe when trust had been shattered.

But underneath it all was fear. I didn't trust anyone else to protect me. Not even God. So, I did it myself.

However, control is a counterfeit safety. It promises peace and delivers anxiety. It keeps us from falling apart, yes, but it also keeps us from healing.

WHAT ARE YOU RUNNING TO?

When we get triggered, we run. That's not weakness—it's survival. Instinctively, we run from the things that remind us of the pain, things that make us feel broken. But what matters is where we run to.

When you're anxious, where do you go?
When you feel pain creeping in, what do you reach for?
When shame whispers, what do you do to shut it up?

For some, it's food—binging or restricting. For others, it's a substance, a toxic relationship, obsessive cleaning, endless scrolling, or disappearing into isolation. It can even look like hyper-productivity or "spiritual busyness."

These things are coping strategies. They are our way of avoiding pain or avoiding God—or both. But eventually, they stop working. All they do is lead us into cycles of addiction, anxiety, shame, and exhaustion.

It matters where we run to when we're triggered. Instead of something temporary to ease what we feel and make us feel better about ourselves for a while, run to prayer, to the one that is eternal. God says,

Matthew 11:28 says,

"Come to me, all of you who are weary and carry heavy burdens, and I will give you rest."

God loves us, and He cares about our struggles, our trauma, and our pain. When we come to Him, we are surrendering our burdens to Him. He can heal us for good, not just temporarily.

THE FEAR BEHIND SURRENDER

Surrender sounds beautiful on paper, but when you've been through trauma, surrender doesn't feel holy. It feels terrifying.

Why? Because we've learned that when we let go, bad things happen.
When we trusted someone, they hurt us.
When we let our guard down, we got used.
When we asked for help, we were rejected.
When we did not restrict food, we got uncomfortable in our body.
So, we made a vow: Never again.

That vow might have kept us alive, but it's also keeping us from freedom.

Surrendering to God doesn't mean we're weak. It means we finally believe that He's strong enough to carry what we can't. It means we're willing to trade control for connection. And that's where the healing begins.

THE DAILY CHOICE TO LET GO

I used to think surrender meant giving up. But in my journey to healing, I've learned that surrender—real surrender—is choosing to let go of what was never mine to carry, and trusting the One who is strong enough to hold it.

Daily surrender isn't just for the moments we feel weak—it's for the moments we think we're strong enough to do it on our own.

The book, *The Genesis Process*, notes that "change comes from doing the opposite of what you feel like doing." That's surrender.

When everything in you wants to restrict, you eat. When everything in you wants to isolate, you reach out. When everything in you wants to numb, you pray—even if all you can say is "help."

Surrender is not a one-time thing. It's a daily practice. Sometimes, even hourly. Surrender is not a finish line—it's a rhythm. A pattern. A practice.

Luke 9:23 says,

Whoever wants to be my disciple must deny themselves and take up their cross daily and follow me.

Not once. Daily.

FALSE SAFETY VS. TRUE SECURITY

Control makes you feel strong, but surrender makes you whole. The safety you build on your own will always be shaky. Trauma tricks us into thinking we can protect ourselves better than God can. But real security comes when we say, "God, I'm terrified, but I trust You more than I trust this pattern."

We can't heal in hiding.
We can't grow in chains.
We can't move forward if our fists are still clenched.

Surrender opens your hands. It says, "I don't know what tomorrow looks like, but I trust the One who holds it."

TRADING COPING FOR COMMUNION

In the early days of my journey to healing, I thought it was enough to say, "God, take this burden away. Take this craving away." But I learned God didn't just want to help me with my burdens; He also wanted to build a relationship with me through it all.

What if we stop asking God to just "take away the craving" and start asking Him to be with us in it? What if we invite Him into the moment we want to restrict, use, run, or shut down?

That's where intimacy is built. That's where the real war is won. We don't overcome addiction by willpower; we overcome it by replacing the false refuge with the real One.

Psalm 9:9 says,

The Lord is a refuge for the oppressed, a stronghold in times of trouble.

151

God doesn't shame us for where we've been running; instead, He invites us into something better.

RECOGNIZING WHEN IT'S TIME TO SURRENDER

Over time, I've learned to recognize the warning signs when I need to surrender again:

- When fear, stress, or anxiety start creeping in
- When I feel the urge to control instead of trust
- When something becomes an idol, something I "need" more than I need God

For example, when my children get sick, panic rises in me. I feel the need to hold on tighter, to "fix" everything myself. That's when I know it's time to surrender them to God, trusting that He loves my children even more than I do.

Or take something small—coffee. At one point, I depended on it just to function. I needed that caffeine to start my day instead of coming to God first. I realized even this needed to be surrendered.

The enemy loves to keep us bound in fear and control. But every time I choose to release my grip, I step into the peace of God.

REFLECTION: LETTING GO OF CONTROL AND RUNNING TO GOD

RESPOND

1. What areas of your life do you still try to control?
2. What fear might be hiding underneath that control?
3. What would it look like to invite God into that space today?

PRACTICING THE TRUTH

Surrender isn't just about letting go—it's about giving God reign over every area of my life. So, I developed my own daily surrender habits.

1. I start my day by inviting Him in: "God, guide me today. Lead me, teach me, and show me Your ways."

2. Then, I declare who He is in my life:

   - You are my Provider.

   - You are my Portion.

   - You are my Healer.

   - You are my Protector.

   - You are my Redeemer.

3. I enthrone Him over my life, not just surrendering, but placing Him at the center of everything. Joshua 1:9 says, "Be strong and courageous, take heart, for the Lord is with you."

Surrender isn't weakness—it's an act of courage.

I used to think strength meant holding it all together. But I've learned that real strength is found in surrender, because it's there, in my letting go, that I've seen God hold me together. He never asked me to be perfect, only to trust Him. And slowly, daily, I do.

JOURNAL PROMPT

What does surrender look like for you today?

Write a letter to God honestly naming the things you've been holding tightly, whether out of fear, pain, or habit. Ask Him to meet you there, show you the root of what you're clinging to, and teach you how to let go.

Remember that this is a safe space. Be honest with God; He already knows.

PRAYER

Father,

You see every part of me, even the parts I've been trying to control on my own. I confess I've been running to things that don't satisfy. I've held on out of fear, but I want to trust You again. Help me surrender—daily, not just once. When fear rises, speak peace. When I try to take things back into my own hands, remind me You are stronger, safer, and better. Teach me how to run to You. Thank You for being a refuge, not a taskmaster. I want to live with open hands.

In Jesus' name,

Amen.

9

Practical Tools for Freedom

–

Coping Skills and Daily Surrender

Freedom is pausing in the middle of craving and choosing a new path.

Healing isn't just spiritual—it's holistic and practical. Yes, Jesus breaks chains in an instant, but He also walks with us as we learn to live in freedom. God doesn't just want your Sunday morning. He wants your Monday afternoon anxiety, your late-night cravings, your trauma flashbacks, and your panic in the pediatrician's office. He's God of every moment.

We've talked about identity, forgiveness, purpose, and surrender. Now let's talk about the tools. Freedom is a journey, and we need them for the road. Not just spiritual declarations, but actual strategies. Not just "pray about it," but "here's what you can do when it hits you." Because the enemy is strategic, and we need to be too.

When I was deep in my struggle with the eating disorder, I didn't just need a reminder of who I was in Christ. I also needed help figuring out what to do when the thoughts came, when I wanted to restrict, and when I felt the familiar tightness in my chest and the numbness crept in.

This is where God meets us—not just in the big spiritual moments, but in the practical ones too.

When I first began walking in healing, I thought I just needed more faith. But the deeper I went, the more I realized that God doesn't just want to change our hearts,

He wants to transform us as a whole. He wants to change our habits. He cares about our thought patterns, our nervous systems, and the little choices we make each day. He's not just the God of breakthroughs; He's the God of the daily process.

GOD IS IN EVERY LAYER OF YOUR HEALING

God met me in random places; it was not always in the same circumstances. He would meet me as I listened to worship music or when I was deep in prayer. But other times, He would meet me when I go for a walk and get into nature, and even when I'm journaling. All these things weren't just ways to pass time—they were sacred. They helped me reconnect with God and experience His peace.

Faith doesn't cancel the need for tools. Faith *empowers* us to use them. God often partners the spiritual with the practical.

Jesus spat on dirt *and* made mud to heal a blind man. He told Naaman to wash seven times in the Jordan. He multiplied loaves *and* had the disciples distribute them. Healing may look like worship music *and* trauma therapy. Like prayer *and* setting boundaries. Like journaling scripture *and* calling a friend before you spiral.

Worship quieted the noise in my mind. Journaling gave language to my pain. Art let me express what I didn't have words for. Nature reminded me of God's beauty and nearness. These practices helped me open my heart again and gave me healthy ways to regulate the chaos inside. And God used these things not just to soothe me, but also to strengthen me.

Don't let shame keep you from reaching for what helps.

THE TOOLS

Freedom doesn't always look like a loud deliverance. Sometimes it looks like pausing in the middle of a craving and choosing a new path. Here are a few tools that helped me in my journey toward healing and freedom with God. I believe they can help others walking through the same things I did—addiction, trauma, or anxiety. These are the tools I've learned to keep close. I don't use them all every day, but I come back to them often. Think of this list as a spiritual survival kit. Use what you need when you need it.

1. Grounding Techniques

When anxiety hits, your nervous system gets hijacked. You can't "just pray it away" when your body is in panic mode. So, breathe. The following methods bring your body back to safety so your mind can follow.

- **5-4-3-2-1 Method:** Name 5 things you can see, 4 you can touch, 3 you can hear, 2 you can smell, and 1 you can taste.
- **Cold Method:** Hold something cold.
- **Deep Breathing:** Take deep belly breaths—inhale through your nose for 4 seconds, hold for another 4 seconds, then exhale slowly for 8 seconds.

2. Create a "Go-To" Scripture List for Common Lies

Write down the lies you hear in your head and speak back with truth found in God's word. Keep these scriptures close—somewhere visible. Speak them out loud. Truth has power.

Examples:

- **Lie:** "I'm too far gone."
  Truth: "He leaves the 99 for the one. Today, I'm the one." (Matthew 18:12-14)

- **Lie:** "This will never change."
  Truth: "He who began a good work in me will carry it to completion." (Philippians 1:6)

- **Lie:** "This temptation is too strong."
  Truth: "With this temptation God has provided me a way of escape." (1 Corinthians 10:13)

3. Distraction + Redirection

Sometimes you don't need to sit in it—you need to *move*. It's not avoidance—it's resisting the enemy with action.

- Go for a walk - even 10 minutes can release endorphins.
- Art and Music - create instead of consume.
- Text a friend - invite someone into your space or join them in there's.
- Acts of kindness - do something for someone else. Freedom grows when we remember our purpose.
- Do a puzzle, drink a glass of water, stretch your body.

4. Journaling with God

This isn't about writing pretty prayers. It's about honesty. Let it be raw. Let it be messy. Let it be real.

- "God, I feel numb."
- "God, I want to restrict today."
- "God, I'm afraid to let go."

Then, listen. Write what you sense Him saying in return. Even if it's just: *I'm still here.*

5. Accountability/Safe Person

You weren't made to fight alone. Whether it's a mentor, a friend, a support group, or a counselor—have someone who knows your battle. Someone who will check in and who will remind you of the truth when you forget.

6. Scripture-Based Visualization

Sometimes, when I can't pray, I *picture* truth.

I picture Jesus walking into my room.
I picture Him sitting with me while I cry.
I picture myself handing Him the thing I can't carry anymore.
I picture Jesus embracing me in a hug when I feel alone.
I picture myself leaning back against Him in a quiet and beautiful hillside, with Him calling me to peace when I feel overwhelmed.
This practice isn't weird—it's biblical.

Psalm 16:8 says,

"I keep my eyes always on the Lord. With Him at my right hand, I will not be shaken."

Let Scripture paint the scene.

7. Set a "First 5" Habit

The first five minutes of your day can shift your whole direction. This practice doesn't take an hour, but it takes intention. Before your feet hit the floor, pause, and then:

- Whisper, "Holy Spirit, lead me today."
- Say one verse out loud.
- Place your hand over your heart and say, "God, I belong to You."

8. Grace Pauses/Delay the Action

Sometimes victory looks like pausing before you react. You can set a timer for 10 minutes to pause, breathe, pray, or journal. Cravings lose power when we create space.

- When you are tempted to restrict: pause and ask, "What am I really needing right now?"
- When shame hits: pause and say, "Jesus, remind me of who I am."
- When anxiety rises: pause and breathe in truth, not panic.

You don't have to get it perfect. You just need to pause. God meets us in that space.

9. Limit Access to Triggers

Pay attention to what feeds your addiction.

- *Social media?*
- *Certain people or environments?*
- *Music, movies, or even certain routines?*

Be honest, and then set boundaries.

10. Celebrate Small Victories

Recovery isn't all or nothing. Celebrate every moment you choose freedom. It matters.

PRACTICAL TIPS FOR INCORPORATING THESE PRACTICES

- *Create a worship playlist* that speaks life and plays truth over your mind.

- *Start a prayer journal*: write your thoughts, prayers, and victories.

- *Use art as a form of expression*: it's not about being perfect, it's about being honest.

- *Get outside*: God speaks through creation. Let Him meet you there.

- *Set boundaries*: name your triggers and invite someone to help you stay accountable.

HONORING GOD THROUGH PHYSICAL HEALTH

When I was in the thick of addiction and trauma, I didn't realize how much my physical health was connected to my mental clarity and emotional stability. I thought food and movement were about appearance, not alignment. But over time, I learned that stewarding my body was never about vanity; it was about vitality. It was about strength for the assignment on my life.

God designed our bodies with intentionality. He made us to move, to rest, to be nourished. And when we neglect those basic needs, everything else suffers—our thoughts get foggy, our patience shortens, and our anxiety increases. But when we care for our physical bodies, we partner with God in the healing process.

This doesn't mean obsessing over calories or chasing unrealistic goals. It means eating enough to fuel your day. It means moving your body because it's a gift, not a punishment. It means knowing that nutrients matter. Vitamins and minerals aren't just for our muscles or bones; they actually affect our brain chemistry, our mood, and our ability to process emotions.

For years, I restricted food in the name of control. I avoided rest because I thought hustle made me holy. But God kept inviting me back to balance. To nourishment. To wholeness.

Taking care of your body is spiritual. It's worship.

Romans 12:1 says,

Therefore, I urge you, brothers and sisters, in view of God's mercy, to offer your bodies as a living sacrifice, holy and pleasing to God—this is your true and proper worship.

Take care of your body, not to be in control, not to impress anyone, but to be ready—strong in body and spirit—for whatever He's called you to.

SIMPLE WAYS TO CARE FOR YOUR BODY WITH GRACE

Here are a few tools that have helped me nourish my physical health, without shame, obsession, or overwhelm:

1.   **Start with gentle movement.**

     You don't have to hit the gym or run a marathon. Start with 10–20 minutes of movement that feels good in your body:

- A walk while talking to God
- Gentle stretching or Pilates
- Dancing with your toddler
- A few squats while dinner's cooking

Movement isn't just about fitness; it can actually help process emotions, reduce anxiety, and lift your mood.

2. **Eat to fuel, not to punish.**

If you've battled restriction or binge cycles, this one can feel tricky. But healing means learning to honor hunger again, and trusting that your body was designed to be nourished.

Try building simple, balanced meals with protein, carbs, and healthy fats. Don't skip meals thinking it's "holy" to deny yourself. Nourishment is not indulgent; it's necessary.

3. **Hydrate like it matters.**

Sometimes we're emotionally or physically exhausted simply because we're dehydrated.

Drinking more water might sound too easy, too banal, but it can impact focus, digestion, and even sleep. It can make us feel better, and when we feel better, we are more ready for his will in our lives.

4. **Supplement wisely, not obsessively.**

There are seasons when your body needs more support, especially postpartum, during stress, or if years of disordered eating have affected your gut. A good multivitamin, omega-3s, or magnesium can make a big difference in mental clarity and emotional stability. But don't obsess; just ask God to guide your choices and take it one step at a time.

5. **Listen to your body and the Holy Spirit.**

Sometimes, fatigue means "move," and sometimes, it means "rest." Sometimes, hunger is physical, and sometimes, it's spiritual. It takes time to discern the difference, but you don't have to figure it out alone. Ask the Lord to teach you how to honor your body again, not for control, but for communion.

YOUR BODY WAS MADE FOR FREEDOM, NOT BONDAGE

The enemy would love for us to stay stuck in cycles of shame about our bodies. He wants us fixated on what our body looks like, what it's been through, and what it can or can't do. But Jesus didn't just die to save your soul; He came to redeem every part of you, including your physical body.

Your body is not the enemy.
Your hunger is not a sin.
Your energy is not a curse.
Your strength is not vanity.

You are a temple of the Holy Spirit, as stated in 1 Corinthians 6:19. And that means your body matters, because He lives in it.

Freedom isn't always perfect habits or meal plans. Sometimes it's eating when you're hungry, resting when you need to, moving your body with joy, and saying, "God, thank You for this vessel You gave me."

When we stop using our bodies to prove something and start using them to praise Him, everything changes.

This is about wholeness.

This is about worship.

This is about walking in the freedom Jesus died to give you.

GOD IN THE EVERYDAY

Healing isn't just spiritual; it's physical, emotional, and practical. And God is in all of it.

He's not disappointed in you when you need help.

He's not absent in your relapse.

He's not waiting for you to get it perfect before He joins you.

He's present at every step of your freedom. He's there in the breath work.

He's there when you get outside and feel the sun on your skin.

He's there in the journaling. In the prayer over panic. In the moment you choose connection over compulsion.

He's Emmanuel—God with you.

REFLECTION: TOOLS FOR FREEDOM

RESPOND

1. Which of these tools stood out to you today?

2. In which area of your life do you think you need these tools the most?

3. Where can you begin to invite God into your patterns?

You don't have to choose between God and tools. He's in the tools. He is "the tool." He's the one who brings healing through prayer and pause, through community and counseling, through truth and tenderness. Don't let the enemy convince you that needing help means you're failing, when it actually means you're healing.

JOURNAL PROMPT

Take inventory of your current coping habits.

Write down:

- What are your most common triggers?

- What do you typically reach for when you're triggered, anxious, or overwhelmed?
- Which of these are helping you heal, and which are keeping you stuck?

Now, ask:

- What would it look like to run to God instead?
- What tool or practice from this chapter do you feel Him inviting you to try or revisit?

PRAYER

Father,

You are my Healer, my Shepherd, and my refuge. Thank You for caring about every layer of my pain: body, mind, and soul. Help me recognize when I'm slipping back into old patterns, and give me the courage to pause and reach for You. I surrender my false comforts and ask You to meet me in the real need underneath. Equip me with Your truth, Your peace, and Your tools to walk in freedom, one day at a time.

In Jesus' name,

Amen.

10

Stumbling into Grace

Just when I thought I was doing fine, I stumbled.

The healing journey isn't a straight line; it's a winding road, filled with beautiful breakthroughs and unexpected detours. Setbacks aren't signs of failure. They are reminders that we're still in process, and that grace is still holding us.

There were moments I thought I had finally "arrived" and that I had outgrown my old patterns and wouldn't return to them again. But healing isn't about arriving—it's about abiding. And abiding means learning to stay close, even when you stumble.

Setbacks used to make me question everything. Was I really free? Did God actually change me? Was I just pretending? But over time, I learned something powerful: Setbacks don't erase your progress. They reveal where healing still needs to happen.

And when we let grace meet us there, those places become the very ground where freedom grows deeper.

WHEN WE FALL, WE DON'T START OVER

I wish I could say I never fell again after I chose victory, but that wouldn't be honest.

About a year into my healing journey, I was already feeling stronger in my walk with God when I began dating someone. One night, he chose to attend a worship night instead of coming to visit me. It wasn't a bad decision, but I didn't see it that way at the time. I felt rejected, unimportant, and brushed aside. So I did what I used to do,

I numbed the pain. I went out, drank, and pretended I was fine. I wasn't. I just didn't want to feel the sadness. I couldn't admit, even to myself, I was still learning how to handle disappointment in a healthy way.

That night wasn't about alcohol; it was about identity. It was about still craving affirmation from people instead of security from God. In the days that followed, I wrestled with shame. But God didn't turn His back on me; He gently turned me back toward Him.

Psalm 103:13-14 says,

"As a father has compassion on his children, so the Lord has compassion on those who fear him; for he knows how we are formed, he remembers that we are dust."

God isn't surprised by our weakness. He meets us there.

GRACE DOESN'T DISQUALIFY YOU

Not long after getting married, I fell again, but in a different way. I had back pain from a previous accident, and I justified using weed and CBD to help me relax before bed.

It felt like no big deal at first, just for pain, nothing abusive. I started feeling convicted, because deep down, I knew it wasn't just about physical pain. It was about control and wanting to self-soothe rather than trust God to comfort me.

During this time, I had a dream that shook me. In the dream, I was waiting in line for a big competition. When they called my name, I approached the front desk, but instead of being welcomed in, I was told I was disqualified. I woke up panicked. What had I done to disqualify myself?

Immediately, the weed came to mind. I realized I had let something else take the place of the Comforter. So I repented. I threw it all away and told God, "I'm sorry I turned to something else instead of You."

In His kindness, He spoke to my heart, not with condemnation, but with a loving reminder: "I'm not upset with you. I just have more for you."

That's the nature of grace. It doesn't ignore sin, but it doesn't define us by it either. It calls us higher. It lifts us out of the pit and reminds us who we really are.

Romans 8:1 says,

"There is now no condemnation for those who are in Christ Jesus."

Not less condemnation, but completely no condemnation. Since then, I've never struggled with falling asleep again. His peace is real.

LEARNING FROM THE SLIP, NOT LIVING IN IT

We don't have to build a house in our setback. We can learn from it, grieve it, repent, and then get back up.

Proverbs 24:16 says,

"Though a righteous man falls seven times, he rises again."

Righteousness isn't perfection; it's the decision to rise again.

Sometimes we think a fall means we're fake or that our healing wasn't real. But that's a lie—one that the enemy wants you to believe. A setback doesn't erase the steps forward you've already taken. It just means you're still in need of grace, and that's true for all of us.

WHEN TRIGGERS TRY TO SNEAK IN

Not every stumble looks like a dramatic fall. Sometimes it starts as a whisper.

A lie.

A trigger.

A moment of stress.

Even now, I sometimes feel the urge to control my body, and the eating disorder thoughts try to creep back in. But they don't stay. God is quicker. He reminds me of who I am and of what I've already walked through. I don't spiral anymore. I just pause, breathe, and speak truth.

2 Corinthians 12:9 says,

> *"My grace is sufficient for you, for my power is made perfect in weakness."*

Weakness isn't a disqualifier; it's an opportunity for His power to show up.

I've learned something important: triggers are often the alarm system that grace wants to answer.

We don't need to fear triggers; we need to recognize them. When fear, stress, or anxiety start creeping in, when you feel the urge to isolate or numb, when you start needing something more than God—that's your signal; it's time to surrender again.

CONVICTION VS. CONDEMNATION

Setbacks used to send me into a shame spiral. But now I know the difference:

- Condemnation says: "You're a failure. You'll never change."

- Conviction says: "This isn't who you are anymore. Let's make it right.

- Condemnation is from the enemy.

- Conviction is from the Holy Spirit.

And that shift in perspective? It's everything.

Romans 8:1 says,

"There is now no condemnation for those who are in Christ Jesus."

We're not disqualified; we're *redirected.*

The key is returning quickly. The longer we stay in shame and condemnation, the harder it is to return. But grace makes a way back every single time.

When we make a mistake, we can run to God, not from Him. We can return quickly, repent fully, and receive the fresh start He offers.

Lamentations 3:22-23 says,

"Because of the Lord's great love we are not consumed, for his compassions never fail. They are new every morning; great is your faithfulness."

Not just once. Every morning.

His mercy doesn't run out. His grace isn't shocked by your journey. He knows it all, and He still chooses you.

JESUS RESTORES THE FALLEN

Peter denied Jesus three times. He swore he didn't even know Him. If anyone should've been disqualified, it was Peter.

But after the resurrection, what did Jesus do?

He cooked Peter breakfast.

He restored him.

He reminded him of his calling: *"Feed my sheep."*

Jesus didn't give up on Peter, and He's not giving up on you.

You didn't ruin your calling.

You didn't lose your worth.

You stumbled.

And He still says, *"Follow Me."*

ACCOUNTABILITY HELPS US STAY FREE

We were never meant to heal alone. One of the most powerful tools in healing is *community*. I've had to learn that when I fall, it is important to share it with others, to invite people into the real version of my story. That doesn't mean blasting it everywhere. It simply means having one or two people who can speak truth when your mind is loud with lies.

When you stumble, don't hide. Tell someone. Find your safe people. Let the light in. That's where shame dies.

HEALING IS LEARNING FROM THE FALL

Instead of asking, "Why did I mess up?", start asking,

"What was I feeling before this happened?"

"Where was I believing a lie?"

"What do I need to surrender?"

We can treat setbacks like shame, or we can treat them like signposts that point us back to Jesus.

GRACE IS GREATER

One bad day doesn't undo the work God has done in you. Your story doesn't lose its power because of a misstep. God is not pacing in heaven, disappointed in you.

He is running toward you. Always.

Proverbs 24:16 says,

"Though the righteous fall seven times, they rise again."

Rising again doesn't mean we're perfect. It means we belong to the One who is.

A DIFFERENT YOU

You're not the same person you were when your story began. Even if you stumble, you now know how to rise. Even if you fall, you fall *forward*, into grace, not shame.

Setbacks don't define you. They simply remind you how deeply you need the One who already claimed you as His.

You're learning how to fight differently. You're not fighting to be free; you're fighting *because* you already are.

REFLECTION

RESPOND

1. Have you ever stumbled in your journey? How did it happen?
2. How long did it take for you to rise again?
3. How did you feel when you come back from your fall? Did you feel like a different or new person?

JOURNAL PROMPT

Think back to a time when you slipped, fell back into an old pattern, or gave in to a coping habit you thought you were past. How did you respond? What thoughts did the enemy try to whisper in that moment, and how does God's truth answer those lies?

Then write this:

"Even when I mess up, God still says ___________."

Let His voice be louder than your shame.

194

PRAYER

Father,

Thank You that grace isn't a one-time gift—it's a daily flood. Thank You that You're not disappointed in me when I fall, but You're always right there to lift me up again.

Help me recognize the difference between condemnation and conviction. When I stumble, remind me who I am in You. Teach me how to learn from my setbacks instead of running from them. And help me see them not as failures, but as moments where grace grows deeper roots.

I surrender the pressure to be perfect. I receive the freedom to be loved, even in my mess.

Thank You for never giving up on me. Thank You that You are making me whole.

In Jesus' name,

Amen.

The Invitation: Come Home

The topics covered in this book are not exhaustive. They're not meant to be the final word on healing, addiction, or trauma; they're meant to be an introduction. A beginning. A gentle nudge toward healing and hope. An invitation.

And the most important invitation of all is this: **Come home.**

I encourage you to find a Bible-believing church community if you're not already a part of one. You were never meant to walk this journey alone.

Maybe you've read these pages and you've never taken that first step of surrender to Jesus. You've heard of Him, maybe even talked to Him, but you've never invited Him to be Lord of your life. Maybe you feel too broken, too far gone, too unworthy.

But here's the truth: **Salvation is not earned. It's a gift.** Freely given. Freely received.

Jesus is not waiting for you to get it all together. He's not holding back until you're "better." He already made a way. He already chose the Cross. And He is calling you now, by name, and with open arms.

Do not drift from grace. Come home.

The great reality of being human is realizing we were born separated from God. And being whole—truly whole—means being restored to Him.

You don't just need temporary comfort. You need something eternal.

You don't just need relief. You need redemption.

You don't just need strength. You need a Savior.

You need Jesus.

In the midst of your pain, God is working to make you whole. To shape you into the person your future requires. To love you right where you are, and never leave you the same.

He is not disappointed in you.

He is not absent in your setbacks.

He's not waiting for perfection; He's offering you grace.

The Bible says in Ephesians 2:8,

"For it is by grace you have been saved, through faith—

and this is not from yourselves, it is the gift of God."

A Prayer to Begin Again

If you're ready to surrender your life to Jesus and step into a relationship with Him, you can pray this simple prayer from your heart.

Jesus, I need You. I can't save myself.

I believe You are the Son of God and that You died for me and rose again.

I ask You to forgive me, to heal me, and to make me new.

I surrender my pain, my past, my shame, and my striving.

I receive Your grace. I receive Your love. I receive the new life You offer.

Be my Savior, be my Lord, be my everything.

I want to follow You for the rest of my life.

Thank You for welcoming me home. Amen.

What Now?

- **Tell someone** about your decision, ideally a believer who can walk with you.

- **Get a Bible** and start reading the Gospels. Start with the Book of John.

- **Find a church** where you can grow, serve, and be surrounded by faith-filled community.

- **Talk to God daily.** You don't need fancy words. Just be honest.

- **Don't give up.** Healing is a journey, and God is walking it with you.

Welcome home.

You're not alone anymore.

Freedom in Christ Declaration

As you walk through your healing journey, it's important to remind yourself daily of who you are in Christ. This declaration is designed to help you speak God's truth over your life, especially in moments of doubt, fear, or weakness. The enemy often tries to attack our identity, but by declaring these scriptural truths, you can stand firm in the freedom and victory Christ has given you.

I encourage you to read or pray this declaration every day. Speak it out loud if possible and let the Word of God take root in your heart. You might want to keep it somewhere you'll see regularly—on your mirror, by your bed, or in your journal—so you can return to it whenever you need a reminder of your identity in Christ.

I am a new creation in Christ.

(2 Corinthians 5:17)

I am fearfully and wonderfully made.

(Psalm 139:14)

I am no longer a slave to fear, addiction, or shame.

(Galatians 5:1)

I am chosen and loved by God.

(Ephesians 1:4-5)

I am forgiven and redeemed.

(Ephesians 1:7)

I am strong in Christ.

(Philippians 4:13)

I have the mind of Christ.

(1 Corinthians 2:16)

I take every thought captive to obey Christ.

(2 Corinthians 10:5)

I am free from condemnation.

(Romans 8:1)

I am God's handiwork, created for a purpose.

(Ephesians 2:10)

I am healed and whole in Christ.

(Psalm 147:3)

I trust in the Lord and lean not on my own understanding.

(Proverbs 3:5-6)

I walk in victory because Jesus has overcome.

(1 Corinthians 15:57)

The same Spirit that raised Christ from the dead lives in me.

(Romans 8:11)

I stand firm in the armor of God and resist the enemy.

(Ephesians 6:13)

I am more than a conqueror through Him who loves me.

(Romans 8:37)

I am in process, but I am never alone. God is faithful to complete the good work He began in me.

(Philippians 1:6)

My story is not over, and neither is yours. God is still writing it—for His glory and our good.

Closing Prayer

Father,

Thank You for meeting us here.

For every page, every memory, every tear, every moment of revelation, You were present.

Thank You for Your healing, for Your patience, and for the grace that has carried us this far.

Lord, I lift up the one reading this.

You see their heart. You know their story, every scar, every silent cry, every battle they've fought in secret.

You are not distant. You are not disappointed.

You are near to the brokenhearted, and You bind up every wound.

Father, I pray that everything they've read would not just remain on these pages, but would take root and bear fruit.

Seal Your truth deep within their spirit. Remind them of who they are in You.

When lies come, let them remember what You've spoken. When shame whispers, let them hear Your song of love louder.

Give them the courage to keep surrendering.

Give them the strength to keep walking, even when it's hard.

Give them peace that passes all understanding.

And give them people, safe people, Spirit-filled people, to walk alongside them.

I pray for complete restoration—body, mind, and spirit.

I pray that this story would just be the beginning. That the healing they've tasted would multiply, spilling into their relationships, their calling, and every corner of their life.

Use their testimony, God. Let their life declare Your faithfulness.

And when they forget, remind them.

When they fall, catch them.

When they feel alone, whisper again: *"You are mine."*

Thank You for being the God who doesn't give up.

Thank You for never wasting pain.

And thank You for what's still to come.

In Jesus' name,

Amen.

ACKNOWLEDGEMENT

Writing a book is a journey—a journey I was thankful I didn't walk through alone. I would be forever grateful to the people who have walked with me even before the idea of this book existed, to those who have helped me turn this book into what it is now, and to the ones who have been with me through my healing journey.

To Page Grey, my editor, thank you for pouring your heart, your prayers, and your perseverance into this book. Even in the midst of your own battles, you faithfully helped me bring these words to life with care and compassion. To Mary Harris, thank you for your encouragement, wisdom, and feedback during the writing process. Your support helped me find my voice on these pages, making me realize that our lives and commitments can impact others in powerful ways.

To Tuff Harris and the One Heart Warriors program, thank you for asking the question that first sparked the idea for this book: "If you could take part in the battle against sex trafficking, what would it look like?" Thank you for challenging me to pray and listen for God's direction. That question opened my eyes to the calling God had placed in me: to speak on identity, to help people heal, and to reach even the hearts that might otherwise turn to abuse.

To Pastors Jerry and Kimberly Dirmann, thank you for creating and leading Jesus Disciple, formerly Operation Solid Lives. Taking your discipleship course had transformed my walk with God and taught me how to build my life on His Word and to lead with boldness.

I am also grateful to the pastor, whom I'd met when I was still new to my healing journey, who once asked me a question that lingered for years and reshaped how I saw myself—you know who you are. That seed God planted through you grew into a powerful shift in my thinking. To Carrie Halloran, who once extended kindness and led me to baptism—you may never know how much your obedience changed the course of my life, but I carry the moments and memories with me always.

To my dad, who never stopped praying for me and always reminded me of the power of prayer. Though you are now with the Lord, your faith continues to live on in me. I am reminded of how near Heaven is when I think of you. You loved to fish, and I loved fishing with you. Now I carry that legacy forward by fishing for souls for Jesus. To my mom, my biggest fan, who fought for me when I couldn't fight for myself. Your love and passion were often the anchors God used to keep me here. To my sisters, thank you for spending countless phone calls listening, encouraging, and walking with me as I talked through this entire process. Your love, patience, and encouragement have meant the world. To my brother, thank you for always being strong for us and providing a safe place to run to.

To my husband, thank you for standing beside me with love and support. You believed in me when I doubted myself, and your faithfulness encouraged me to keep going. To my children, who remind me daily of God's redemption and the joy of new beginnings. You are living proof that beauty can come from ashes.

To my extended family and friends, thank you for your prayers, encouragement, and for standing beside me in both seasons of pain and joy. Your faith and love have carried me farther than you know.

Above all, I thank my Lord and Savior, Jesus Christ. He is the Author of redemption, the One who gave me a voice, and the reason these pages exist. This book is part of my casting the net, trusting Him to draw hearts to Himself. To Him be all the glory.